D1627506

CHECKED

RIDLEY
SCOTT

Already a highly successful commercials director, Ridley Scott decided to become a film director in the early 1970s. 'I realized how bad so many films were. I was frustrated by what I was seeing in theatres and decided to go into movies myself.'

RIDLEY SCOTT

Paul M. Sammon

ORION

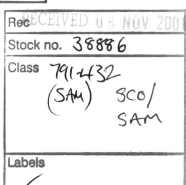

For my mother CATHERINE MARIE DOANE SAMMON who led me to my seat in the temple of cinema

First published in 1999 by Orion
An imprint of Orion Books Ltd
Orion House, 5 Upper St Martin's Lane, London WC2H 9EA

Copyright © Paul M. Sammon 1999
Project editor: Natasha Martyn-Jones

A CIP catalogue record for this book is available from the British Library.

Reproduction by Pixel Colour Ltd, London
Printed in Italy by Printer Trento srl.
Bound by L.E.G.O., Vicenza

CONTENTS

Acknowledgements

It goes without saying that this volume would not be possible without the films of Ridley Scott. But neither would I have had such a good time writing it, if not for the always gracious manner of the man behind those motion pictures.

Since 1980 (the year we first met), Ridley Scott has consistently agreed to my every interview request with candour and respect. Moreover, this formidably gifted film-maker continues to tolerate my sporadic disruptions of what I know is one of the most demanding schedules in the entertainment business. So for all that, Ridley, my utmost thanks. I very much enjoyed our conversations (though I'm not so sure about those cigars), and hope you'll agree that this final section of my unofficial 'Ridley Scott triptych' (*Future Noir* and *The Complete Aliens* being its other two panels) does proper justice to your work.

Still, I do regret that *Ridley Scott: The Making of His Movies* does not fully reflect the qualities I most admire about its subject. Mr Scott's sense of humour, his thoughtfulness and unpretentiousness, are rare enough in the ordinary world – to find such qualities in the fields of global advertising and Hollywood film-making is simply astonishing... and so noted.

Of nearly equal importance to the assembling of this book have been the efforts of Anne Lai, Ridley Scott's L.A. assistant. Ms Lai's talents, diligence and lack of attitude are fully the equal of her employer's; Anne is also a rock of stability in an ocean of insanity, and without her commendable steadiness, this effort probably would have driven me mad quite some time ago. Thanks for everything, Anne, on every project – you are indeed the consummate professional. My appreciation also goes to Julie Payne, Ridley's London assistant, and to Neville Shulman, Mr Scott's long-term advisor and business manager.

Analogous gratitude to Trevor Dolby, my Orion editor. You knew exactly how to make this project a (nearly) stress-free experience, Trevor, and I very much appreciated that. Additional thanks for thinking of me in the first place.

Similar acknowledgements to Pandora White, also of Orion, for her help.

To Harry Bromley-Davenport – director, producer, bon vivant, friend – belated but sincere gratitude for snatching me away from the slough of despond. Your steadfast support and faith in my talents (whatever those might be) came at a time I most needed them. I'll never forget our good times, Harry – or that nightmare in Texas!

As for Lori Perkins, my agent, whom I will always treasure for seeking me out, these few but telling words: eight down, and counting.

Finally, to Sherri Sires Sammon, wife and 23-year-long companion – who probably thinks I've run out of things to say – I haven't, sweetheart. Not by a long shot. You'll never know the depth of my indebtedness to you, or how much I've respected your uncountable sacrifices and treasured the ways you've enriched my life. I thank you, now, while I'm still able. Always remember, whatever comes tomorrow, that I never regretted a moment of our time together. And to hell with any other role model – you're the paradigm, kid.

I stand in fucking awe.

'If you apply pure logic to your choice of subject, that's dangerous. Potentially sterile. So to a certain extent you're drawn into a film by your own instincts. And I think that my instincts happen to be fairly commercial ones.'

The Man With the Golden Eye

Ever since the first, optically ravishing examples of his art burst upon world cinema in 1977, the films of Ridley Scott have, more often than not, been touched by paradox.

Consider: *The Duellists* was a beautifully textured debut that energetically explored one manifestation of male 'honour' by amplifying it to an extraordinary degree. It also received excellent notices (for its thematic fidelity to the Joseph Conrad story on which it was based), and elicited critical raves for its remarkable, Dutch Master-like imagery. Yet Scott's first feature film was little seen, and even more poorly marketed.

Ridley Scott's next two productions unarguably became *the* seminal influences on the look and tone of countless science fiction pictures to come. Still, at the time of their release, *Alien* and *Blade Runner*'s most impressive qualities – their spare, elliptical narratives and astonishing production designs – polarized audiences and critics alike.

Next came *Legend*, Scott's baroque valentine to the innocence of myth. The film incontestably boasted what were perhaps the most staggering images captured within a 1980s-era soundstage – yet *Legend* then went on to become one of the few films starring Tom Cruise *not* to make money.

Nevertheless, Scott's career continued, and flourished. *Someone to Watch Over Me*, *Black Rain*, *Thelma and Louise* – all these and more were 'Directed By Ridley Scott'. At the same time, this most unpredictable of mainstream film-makers continued to generate divergent reviews. Some commentators wrote Scott off as an elitist, too narrowly focused director; others were impressed by how he always worked with major studios, and the biggest stars. A small-ish set of critics (rightly) viewed Scott as one of the most respect-ed 'players' within the notoriously competitive motion picture industry; dissenting reviewers (erroneously) concentrated on the downside of a track record that contained setbacks and success.

And over everything hovered this superficial, oft-repeated refrain: Ridley Scott was more style than substance. A film-maker so intoxicated by the voluptuous possibilities of the visual, that his delirious images frequently overwhelmed narrative and character-ization.

Scott's loyal fans, however – and he has many – totally refute that position. Ridley Scott, the contend, is one of the few film directors to whom audiences will continue to relate and from whom they expect high filmic quality, which goes far towards explaining the longevity of this 'director with the golden eye'. Still, that 'style vs. substance' argument possibly explains why – even though cin-ema historians have had twenty-odd years to do otherwise – *Ridley Scott: The Making of His Movies* is the first book-length study of the films of Ridley Scott. And this during a period when the most aes-thetically threadbare exploitation directors already have had mul-tiple volumes devoted to their *'oeuvres'*.

However, it is rather easy to see why many critics have never seriously studied Scott's work. First comes the nature of his early career. Throughout the mid Sixties and early Seventies, Ridley Scott initially gained eminence as a strikingly successful director of sophisticated British television commercials – he personally produced, directed and photographed literally *thousands* of such spots. But although directing commercials is now considered an acceptable training ground for nascent feature directors, such was not always the case, and serious critics still do not exactly race to embrace the *auteur* of the latest sliced bread advert. Instead, they prefer reflexively to pigeonhole film-makers with advertising back-grounds as camera-happy technicians interested only in the visu-al. How that superficial judgement must have seemed justified, once Scott founded Ridley Scott Associates, today among the world's most influential advertising production companies!

Further critical misgivings have been raised by the fact that Scott's feature films are very much a product of the Hollywood stu-dio system. This harsh environment, most critics argue, is guaranteed to suffocate individual expression; moreover, the commercial blockbusters generated within that system – such as *Alien*, Scott's biggest 'event' film – are also automatically suspect, since any motion picture that generates rapturous world-wide success *must* do so by pandering to the lowest common denominator.

Finally, some critics find fault with Scott's growing status as a mini-mogul. For Scott is indeed a burgeoning tycoon, one who not only supervises (with brother Tony) his own production company, but who is also the owner (again with Tony) of a motion picture development company (Scott Free), a major European studio (Shepperton), and a respected special effects house (The Mill).

With his history so closely tied to commerce, then, it should come as no surprise that many pundits view Ridley Scott as too successful, too technical, or too mercantile to take seriously. For these critics, Scott is the literal embodiment of the term 'commercial director', and no other description guarantees such instant academic anathema.

However, might I suggest that the preceding observations are not only themselves superficial, but almost laughably obtuse? Many of the same critics who put forward these views seem to forget that they themselves were weaned on *Cahiers du Cinéma*, a French film magazine that generated an influential school of criticism which, in turn, routinely *championed* such formerly dismissed Hollywood directors as Howard Hawks, Bud Boetticher and Robert Aldrich. Moreover, such reassessments were created by writers willing to examine the *entire body of a director's work*, and to patiently sift through film after film while staying on the alert for common themes, obsessions, and motifs.

Such cinematic archaeology, in fact, remains the most effective method for deciding whether one's subject has the personal signature of an uncommon artist, or the anonymous imprint of an impersonal hack.

As you will soon see, *Ridley Scott: The Making of His Movies* – despite the current consensus to the contrary – arrives at the former conclusion.

This book is based on over 100 hours of taped, mostly in-person interviews which I have conducted with Ridley Scott since 1980. During that period, we discussed each of his completed films at length (up through *G.I. Jane*), plus some that had fallen by the wayside. Inevitably, a few of our sessions yielded hitherto little-known facts that, upon closer examination, helped better define the personal pulse throbbing beneath Scott's films.

One was his early interest in documentary film-making. This impulse towards street-level realism clearly has been an influence on the naturalistic performances and believable characters that typically frequent Scott's features, no matter how fantastic their surroundings. Another was the director's fondness for developing his own projects. A third linked Scott to certain other notable, immensely talented, but frequently misunderstood 'auteurist' directors – for Ridley Scott often directs, produces, designs, has a strong influence on the writing of, and at times even photographs, each of his own motion pictures, only to see some of his best work mutilated by uncomprehending studios or producers.

Of course, any attempt to alter Scott's status from that of talent-ed hired gun to unique artist must begin with an examination of the signatory methods he's utilized to create that art. Therefore, to commence with the obvious, let's start with the visual.

Scott's cinematic style is typically ornate, sophisticated and state-of-the-art. This optical dexterity did not evolve in a vacuum, however; instead, it can be traced back to any number of individ-ualistic traits. For example, the highly energetic, at times fiery-tempered Scott possesses a passionate fondness for, and deep understanding of, modern, classical and popular art (his first four films, in fact, build entire sequences around the 'looks' of Vermeer, Edward Hopper, Francis Bacon, Arthur Rackham, H.R. Giger and Rembrandt). Scott is also a talented graphic artist, who routinely draws and/or paints finely crafted sketches, paintings and story-boards to communicate what he's after during each particular film. In addition, Scott 'thinks pictorially', as he once put it to this writer.

Such a talent must connect with the fact that Ridley Scott began his professional career as an art director. This intimate under-standing of how cinematic sets and props are created (and how best to present those items on the studio floor) has served Scott very well, resulting in motion pictures that are exactingly, even obses-sively, detailed. But Scott is not only adept at manipulating physi-cal objects within the frame, he is also an acknowledged master of photographic lighting techniques (a veritable 'Lord of Light'), and has so expanded upon the basic lessons learned as an art director that he now 'designs' virtually *every element* of 'a film by Ridley Scott' – every set, camera move, prop, lens, performance, editing strategy and sound. Furthermore, he routinely goes to great lengths to ensure that each of these pieces are precisely fitted together, demonstrating the same sort of elegant attention to detail as a master Venetian painter or classic English lithographist.

Other technical commonalities in the films of Ridley Scott include a repeated use of striking compositions and unusual angles, his frequent reliance on frontlight/backlight techniques (whereby high contrast backlighting is combined with softer, filtered illumination that simultaneously frontlights the performers), and Scott's always-mobile camerawork. This is a director who also tends to rely on recurring, Neo-Expressionistic motifs – heavily smoked sets, dark, brooding exteriors and dusky rooms pierced by shafts of blinding white light.

Yet before I am accused of simply listing a register of the same technical devices that critics often accuse Scott of overusing, it should be emphatically noted that Scott's mastery of the visual has not resulted in the same dramatically empty, superficial 'flash' so apparent in some of the work of imagistic directors such as Alan Parker and Adrian Lyne. Indeed, unlike other 'purely perceptual' film-makers, Scott possesses the virtue of repeatedly seeking out, and having a preference for, superior literary material on which to ground his films.

Such an assertion, of course, flies in the face of the popular notion that Ridley Scott has little understanding of conventional narratives. 'But that's quite not true,' offers one collaborator, who's worked beside Scott on numerous films. 'Ridley is actually always concerned about story, and he usually picks a good one. If anything, it's his tendency to constantly keep changing things, to endlessly add new twists and wrinkles to those stories, until they hardly resemble what Ridley started with, that gets him into trouble.'

While this author cannot bear witness to Scott's tendency constantly to alter his material, he *can* testify to the fact that the director does indeed have a great respect for story, dialogue and characterization. Scott usually spends months with his writers reworking the scripts of his films, until he's satisfied that they're ready to go before the camera. Additionally, he often pursues only the best writing talent; for example, mainstream novelist Joseph Conrad and paranoid science fiction author Philip K. Dick have both had their fiction adapted by Ridley Scott, while the director routinely collaborates with some of the film industry's brightest, most talented screenwriters (Walter Hill, David Webb Peoples, William Hjortsberg). One could argue that it's the *way* Scott presents his stories that results in his being accused of not understanding narrative – but more on that in a moment.

The mere fact that Ridley Scott has good taste in screenwriters would mean nothing, of course, if he then shot their scripts without contributing his own personality. Thankfully, Scott does bring a unique sensibility to his work. Some call this characteristic 'European' – I prefer 'mature'. Scott has consistently pulled off the difficult narrative trick of making his pictures fit comfortable generic parameters (the historical picture, the crime thriller, the science fiction movie, the action film, etc.), while simultaneously adding challenging subtexts that repeatedly address serious, real-world concerns. A simple plot summary of *Blade Runner*, for instance, might read 'detective in the future'; however, this is a film that also raises questions of identity, celebrates empathy, and reminds us of the value of life – all life. To take another example, *Someone to Watch Over Me* nominally positions itself as an urban crime picture, yet it is staged against (and comments upon) an America stratified by a very real class system, while simultaneously examining the disorienting impact an extramarital affair wreaks upon a hitherto stable marriage. And though *Black Rain* may play like an exotic, Japanese *yakuza* thriller, it is actually about honour, loyalty and redemption.

It is exactly this point – that Ridley Scott's pictures are always about something – that sets them apart from their equally well-made, but more superficial, kin. Time and again one discovers hidden undertones in the work of Ridley Scott: for example, the way *Legend*'s virtuous Tom Cruise is seduced into a terrible misjudgement by the 'innocent' Mia Sara (who plays upon Cruise's vanity and desire). Or the manner in which Thelma and Louise's apparently liberating attempts to break away from a lifetime of female stereotyping actually lead them down a dead-end road. Other instances also exist, but the point has been made – Ridley Scott's motion pictures are not empty exercises in technique. On the contrary, they often are suffused with a faint, but nonetheless quite genuine, whiff of social criticism.

Scott then fleshes out these intriguing undercurrents by typically casting skilled, up-and-coming actors to populate his films. Which raises another point; not many people seem to realize that it is primarily Ridley Scott who cast in his films and 'discovered' such talents as Sigourney Weaver, Daryl Hannah, Michael Madsen, Michael Wincott and Brad Pitt. Even fewer grasp Scott's exceptional skill at guiding his performers through unaffected, naturalistic performances. (As Sigourney Weaver once told this writer, 'Ridley has a very good nose for sniffing out whatever's false in human behaviour'.) And Scott's subtle storytelling methods – his films often unfold obliquely, elliptically, through inference and suggestion – also usually escape attention.

No matter. Scott's methods have remained constant, as you will discover in this book. You will also encounter an artist – yes, artist – who expects us to understand what he's about and to know what his films are about, even as he crafts the sort of big, brilliantly polished product today's Hollywood seems so intent on ramming down our throats. But while Scott may indeed fashion mainstream movies, he at least makes them for grown-ups – and he never talks down to his audience. And a careful review of Scott's output also reveals commonalities, obsessions and motifs.

So while Ridley Scott may not overtly possess the intellectual credentials of the late Stanley Kubrick, or even demonstrate the same fondness for cinematic trivia exhibited by 'megabuffs' like Martin Scorsese or Quentin Tarantino, his ongoing films, as well as his formidable technical skills, obvious flair and individuality (no other film quite looks or plays out like one directed by Scott) clearly marks him as a director worthy of serious evaluation.

It is in the spirit of that last statement, then – plus its attempt to inform the casual film buff of the production histories behind Scott's often dazzling, sometimes maddening, always unique motion pictures – that *Ridley Scott: The Making of His Movies* now begins.

1 South Shields and the RCA

Ridley Scott was born to Elizabeth and Francis Percy Scott, in South Shields, Tyne and Wear, England, on 30 November 1937. He was the second of three brothers. Frank, the eldest, died of cancer in 1980; Tony (six years younger than Ridley) is the director of such films as *Top Gun* (1986), *Crimson Tide* (1995) and *Enemy of the State* (1998).

South Shields, Ridley's birthplace, is located on the cold, harsh, northeastern edge of England, an area whose inhabitants are routinely described as tough, industrious and taciturn. Yet Scott today has nothing but fond memories of his youth. He recalls the closely knit, middle-class English household into which he was born as being 'conventional, but supportive. I think my parents were very traditional, and gave me a very traditional upbringing. Because it very solid, my childhood became a huge confidence builder. My parents never said no to anything in terms of what I really cared about or had a talent for. Instead they'd say, "If that's what you want to do, great. It's what you do best."'

The earliest years of Scott's life were marked by an unusual mixture of influences – commerce, ships, the military and travel. During the 1930s, Francis Percy (better known to the family as 'Frank') had been a partner in a successful shipping business based in Newcastle. This firm had dealt with much of the commercial shipping then originating from Scandinavia; however, the outbreak of World War II, and the ever-present danger of prowling German U-boats, essentially put an end to this phase of the senior Scott's life.

'There was no business and nobody knew how long the war

would go on,' Scott recalls. 'So Dad got a job in the Army and became a commissioned officer. In fact, during the last two years of World War II, he was attached to the War Office, and associated with Churchill. He also spent time working on an operation named Mulberry Harbour, helping to get our troops successfully into Normandy.'

Francis Percy Scott 'loved the military', says his son, and not long after the end of the war, the Scott clan embarked on the sort of quasi-rootless lifestyle still common to military families. Ridley Scott found himself travelling to, and living in, such varied locations as London, Cumbria and Wales, and the Scott family also resided in Germany from 1947 to 1952. Scott's father then retired from the military and returned to Stockton-on-Tees in northeast England, where he again took up the shipping business.

The self-discipline and constant travel associated with the military would serve Ridley well in his later years, particularly as both elements are so inherently part of the modern film-maker's lifestyle. Yet while Scott's character was being moulded by wars, travel and the shipping business, he also became aware of a strong artistic streak running through his family. 'I remember as a kid my father was great with a pen and black ink,' Scott says. 'He'd do drawings, and he might even have started me off. Because by the time I was six or seven, I was always drawing ships and horses.'

By all accounts, Scott's earliest doodlings revealed hints of the gifted visual stylings he would later bring to his motion pictures.

I loved sketching and discovering artists and reading the comic strips, [Scott explains] almost to the exclusion of everything else. One of the things I'd do was closely examine the *frames* of a comic strip. I'd look at the corners of a room in a comic panel, then the pictures on the walls, then the positioning of the characters, then the lighting effects that had been drawn in by the illustrator. From the beginning, I always found myself drawn to dark, rather melancholy subjects. In fact the comic that used to freak me out more than anything was *Little Orphan Annie,* and not just because Annie had no friends, but because her strip dealt with such gloomy subjects – poverty, violence, orphans. Back then, *Annie* was a very dark strip.

While exploring the worlds of high art and pop culture, Scott was concurrently enjoying another childhood diversion – motion pictures. 'I used to like going to the cinema,' Scott says. 'But it was all rather ordinary, you know? At that point in my life, it wasn't as if films were the great passion of my life. I'd go with my family or mates and sit in the dark and watch whatever was playing that week. What I most remember was the sense of community back then. If a musical was playing, I'd sit there with a bag of popcorn and sing along with the rest of the kids. If it was a thriller, I'd shout, "Look out behind you!", along with everyone else. I think we've lost that innocent sense of audience participation today.'

In spite of his supportive home life and evolving personal interests, however, the young Ridley Scott was also educationally lacking.

Academically, my life was kind of disastrous. I was simply uninterested in traditional educational subjects. In the community I was brought up in, that was a liability. One was raised to believe that the best goal in life was to get a good education, then become a teacher. Earning something like a doctorate was the peak of local ambition. Becoming a lawyer was super peak. But none of that appealed to me.

However, there was one teacher in a school I was attending that I really liked. His name was Mr Cleeland. I remember him to this day. I liked him, I think, because he was a 'neomaster', a young blood in what was otherwise a stuffy grad school. Anyway, one day, right out of the blue, he said, 'You shouldn't be going to the 'sixth' (the final stages of English grad school). 'Instead, you should go to art school. Because that's what you do best.' And I instantly knew that that was the answer for me, because I wasn't particularly academic. I wasn't stupid. I just didn't like it, and if you don't like something, you don't take it in.

Scott took his perceptive teacher's suggestion home to his parents. They were, as always, completely supportive of their son's interests, so Scott then applied to, and was accepted in 1954 by, the West Hartlepool College of Art. This institution was located about 30 miles south of South Shields in the seaside town of Hartlepool, in the north east of England.

Mr. Cleeland had one last parting shot for me before I went to art school, [continues Scott]. First he said something like, 'Well, if you're going to West Hartlepool, you'll probably end up teaching.' And you know, after graduation,

I did indeed receive a National Diploma from West Hartlepool (in graphic design) that would have enabled me to teach. At least in England. But Cleeland then said something else that was much more interesting. I'd been doing a lot of painting, and Cleeland told me, 'Whatever you do, don't go into painting. Because if you do, you're going to end up as a weekend painter, and be desperately unhappy. Try something else, like designing posters. Commercial posters. There's money in that.'

Now, this was 1954, remember. England was only really just getting started with the advent of television, so there was no commercial advertising in the UK. Not on TV, anyway, there were no commercial channels. There was only the BBC, right? Which was totally state-funded. So I tucked away Mr Cleeland's advice and went off to West Hartlepool.

Scott spent four years at art college, during which time he assiduously studied drawing and sketching. He also excelled at painting, although did not confine himself to it. However, the most important door West Hartlepool opened for Ridley Scott was a deeply personal one.

'As soon as I went to art school, I adored it,' Scott fondly recalls. 'I basically lived in that place. I'd do five days a week, then I'd do five nights a week, all in the same five days. I did that for four years. And so I found passion.'

The adolescent under-achiever had now blossomed into a serious, increasingly proficient artist. Yet Scott recalls that not everyone shared his newfound enthusiasm.

I still recall running into someone after I'd done my four years at West Hartlepool who I'd known earlier, a man who'd gone on to become a lawyer. We sort of bumped into each other at a tennis club and this very middle-class attorney said, 'So – you're still pushing a pencil?' I was angered by that. But I just looked at him and said, 'Yes. It's going all right.'

What he did not understand was that being brought up under art training is not about pushing pencils. Because while I was at West Hartlepool, I suddenly became very conscious of music, for example, and writing and other topics. I'd begun to see how they all interrelated with art. I'd also started to become aware of how I saw things personally, how I viewed the world. So the whole process opened up.

Surprisingly, part of this process turned Scott away from the inter-

est that had originally led him to art college – painting. For despite
the praise his canvases brought from teachers and peers, the young
Scott found himself slowly drifting away from the world of brushes
and easels during his years at West Hartlepool. Instead, he began
focusing on the disciplines of still photography and graphic design.
'Perhaps I was subconsciously acting on the advice of my grad
school teacher, Mr Cleeland' Scott recalls today, 'since these new
interests were taking me a step closer to designing posters.'

In 1958, Ridley Scott graduated from the West Hartlepool
College of Art. He was now twenty years old; he had pursued his
studies so diligently that he matriculated as an Honours Student,
an accomplishment that would have eased his transition into the
postgraduate arena, had he decided to continue his studies. Yet at
this point Scott was in no hurry to further his education – at least
academically.

'I'd just done four years of real brainbashing in art school. And
loved it, but now I had the opportunity to step back for two years
and do National Service. I was still rather fascinated by the military, so I decided to enlist in the Marines. I figured, well, if I'm
going to do two years of conscription, I may as well do something
physical. But my father stopped me. He said, "No. Go back to art
school. That's what you do well. Stick with it." So I decided, OK,
I'll give art school another try. For a while. *Then* I'll do my two
years. But that never happened.'

The event which deflected Scott away from military service was
a generous scholarship offered by the Royal College of Art. This
prestigious, London-based institute was – and is – one of the
United Kingdom's most respected postgraduate facilities, special-
izing in art and design. Moreover, Scott was also aware of the RCA's
reputation as a vital, extremely progressive institution. Therefore,
he applied to and was accepted by the RCA in 1958.

'I spent three fantastic years at the Royal College,' Scott says of
the experience. 'I went in specifically as a graphic designer. But
what was particularly good about the RCA was that it allowed you
to move around and investigate different areas. I used to build a
sculpture, do some photography, look in on the school of industrial design. Do a bit of this, and a bit of that. The RCA was an
incredibly stimulating, well-rounded environment.'

While at the Royal College of Art, Scott also continued to study drawing, an interest that had been with him since childhood. Interestingly, the director still draws and paints today, and, as Scott points out, 'these abilities are invaluable to the film-making process. One sketch is infinitely more useful than the best two-hour story conference.'

But to get back to the RCA, by the time I'd earned my diploma there in graphic design, I'd decided that really wasn't what I wanted to do. Because by now television was gaining ground in England, and I liked the idea of designing sets for that medium. So I did two extra postgraduate courses in my last year at the RCA. One was set design, which was then called Theatre Design. That was run by a very interesting guy, called George Haslam, who was a practising theatre and television designer. He was good at what he did, and was also on the cutting edge of television at that point. George took us through the fundamentals of theatre and TV, and basically taught us how to read a play.

I was doing all this, [Scott concludes] because I'd figured that such courses would help ease me into the world of television and film work, which in those times, at least for someone like me, was very mysterious. There was really no specific English school teaching film in the early 1960s, except for technicians. It seemed like the only way someone could work in Hollywood was if you happened to be born in California, or if your dad was in the film industry.

Scott's interest in film had been stimulated by a remarkable upheaval in world-wide cinema that erupted during the late Fifties and early Sixties, and which effectively transformed the art form. This startling, seemingly unstoppable torrent of fresh motion pictures had resulted in the French New Wave, the Italian Neo-Realist movement, and the English 'Angry Young Man'/'Kitchen Sink' school of film-making. Scott, as a young, gifted art student studying at one of Europe's most progressive colleges, could not help but be aware of this phenomenon; however, by the future director's own admission, he also had not fully appreciated film's *creative* possibilities – until now.

I really only became a hardcore movie buff, in a serious fashion, when I came to the RCA and London. Then I used to spend every weekend in the National Film Theatre or places like the Academy Cinema on Oxford Street, where I was suddenly seeing all types of cinema. Japanese, French, Indian films, all of that.

At the time I was the biggest fan of Ingmar Bergman, and still am. The first film I ever saw of Bergman's was called *Summer with Monika* (1953), which was absolutely brilliant. Just the sensitivity and reality of it, the authenticity of the actors and the story, which was so – well, mundane is the wrong word – but naturalistic, perhaps. It was just about life, you know? And I'd never seen a film dramatize life like that before. I thought it was very interesting.

At the same time, [Scott adds with a chuckle] I'd also always been a big fan of Hollywood. In fact, the thing I wanted to do most of all during art school was make a western!

The second major circumstance cementing Scott's new career choice was actually something of an accident. While rummaging around in a cupboard at the RCA's Theatre Design department, Scott stumbled across an old 16mm camera. This was a spring-wound Bolex, complete with a light meter and instruction manual.

'The Royal College did not have a film school at that point,' says Scott. 'They only had their Theatre Design department. But George Haslam got the college to allocate his department at least one camera and a light meter.'

Fired with enthusiasm over his discovery, Scott decided to make the best possible use of this new tool by utilizing the Bolex to make his first film. By necessity, this project would have to be a home-grown one. After signing out for the camera and setting aside the munificent sum of approximately £65 (roughly $100) for film stock, sound recording and processing, Scott studiously devoured the Bolex's operational manual.

Once he felt comfortable with the mechanics of his discoveries, Scott next wrote a short screenplay entitled *Boy and Bicycle*. This detailed the adventures of an average youngster, who decides to skip school by spending the day exploring a small seaside town on his bike. What was interesting about this initial scenario – particularly in light of Scott's later reputation as a film-maker favouring image over verbiage – was the extraordinary amount of dialogue Scott wrote for *Boy*.

'Actually, it was all stream of consciousness,' Scott explains, 'which I intended to do as voice-over. And there was a lot of it. But in those days I was very much into the literature of James Joyce and Henry Miller, who used interior dialogue to great effect; for example, I loved the stream of consciousness in *Ulysses*. So the stream of consciousness I wrote for *Boy and Bicycle* very much came out of the sort of literary background I was noodling and fiddling around with back then.'

According to Scott, literature also influenced *Boy and Bicycle*'s plot. '*Boy* really has no story. It's just an incident. I wanted to do something more literary than just a straightforward narrative, something along the lines of an isolated adventure. Therefore, I came up with the idea of a boy playing hooky, of taking a day out to find that he's suddenly isolated and outside of his own idea of the law. Where suddenly he can't talk to anyone. *Boy and Bicycle* is really about isolation, and isolation in a youth.'

The 27-minute film that Scott ultimately made opens with a young lad named Tony (played by Scott's then 16-year-old brother, Tony Scott) waking up in his bed on the morning of his sixteenth birthday. Tony then lets his gaze roam idly over the familiar furnishings of his cosy bedroom, while ruminating about 'what it means to be a man'. Next the off-screen voices of Tony's parents impatiently tell him to come down for breakfast.

After a quick cut, Tony is seen pedalling his bicycle through the narrow byways of his English home town, as a constant stream of observations and images wash over the viewer. We hear Tony decide to cut class for the day; witness him cycling through nearly empty streets; see him go into a candy store; watch as he pauses at the seashore for a 'fag' (cigarette); eavesdrop as Tony passes through a deserted amusement park (where he muses on how the battered wooden horse atop a small merry-go-round 'would be scary, if it came to life').

Eventually, Tony's aimless wanderings lead him to a dreary, swamp-like, seemingly isolated beach. The gloomy skies overhead begin leaking a thin drizzle. Tony looks for a place of shelter. He stumbles across the carcass of a large dog, rotting in the mud (this genuine dead dog, a German Shepherd, 'just happened to be there'). Then, while wheeling his bike through the clinging muck, Tony discovers a forlorn jetty littered with rickety huts.

Tony breaks into one of these shacks. It is deserted. Deathly quiet. Tony is surprised to discover that apparently the ramshackle hovel is, or at least recently has been, inhabited. The boy wanders through the hut's cramped rooms, discovering a table, bed, books.

Tony has found some fading photographs of elderly women, and is ruminating on his own mother, when a slight breeze unexpected-ly blows through the shack. The draft causes the eye of a dirty doll (with a smashed face) to seemingly wink at the boy. Then a thun-derclap booms overhead. Tony is suddenly frightened. He races to the door – but his way is blocked by the gaunt figure of the hovel's owner, a shabbily dressed, thin-faced tramp. This apparition has apparently returned home, unobserved. He glares at the boy.

Tony manages to dodge around the vagrant and races outside. He grabs his bike and runs off with it into the distance, as the still-staring tramp silently watches him disappear down the beach.

Shot in high-contrast 16mm black and white, *Boy and Bicycle* was very much a family affair. Not only did brother Tony perform as the lead, but Scott's father Francis portrayed the wordless, men-acing vagrant, while Elizabeth Scott was given a brief cameo as the fictional Tony's mother. Ridley produced, wrote and directed; he also storyboarded the entire short ('every frame'), edited the film, and served as its cameraman. The embryonic director also used various technical tricks to enhance the look of his project.

'I adored Kurosawa at that point,' Scott recalls, 'and knew he used certain filters for his monochrome films. So I was stuffing on red filters every chance I got. That, of course, made the skies go black. I also wanted to shoot *Boy and Bicycle* freed from the tripod. So I used a lot of hand-held camera, and even drafted my father to act as a camera-car driver. One day I got Dad to drive around my old stamping grounds at West Hartlepool (all of *Boy* was shot with-in two miles of that town's Art College) in front of Tony on his bike. I sat in the trunk, filming him.'

Despite its humble origins, *Boy and Bicycle* is surprisingly sophisticated for a first effort. It exhibits an abundance of atmos-phere, fluid, assured cinematography, and striking compositions (of the towns, factories, railroad yards and seashore arcades sur-rounding West Hartlepool). *Boy* also benefits from a quasi-docu-mentary, quasi-experimental approach; the relaxed, convincing performance given by Tony Scott is another asset.

But *Boy and Bicycle* is also, it must be remembered, an amateur effort, prone to the missteps and indulgences abundant in many first films (particularly those with such a tiny budget). Its greatest liabilities are its 'plot' (which could have benefitted from some judicious trimming), and Tony's staccato, never-ending, pseudo-poetic monologues. However, his arch stream of consciousness *is* used to good effect. For instance, when Tony is in the vagrant's hut and finds a photograph that reminds him of his mother, a jumpcut immediately takes us to a mirrored reflection of Elizabeth Scott, while the boy mentally 'says', 'She looks just like Mum. Wonder what they laughed at and where they went afterwards. She's just like Mum you know, like that photo in the album at home. I can remember certain moments very clearly, little things, pointless really. The tiny cut-glass salt cellars at Mrs Smith's, in Harton. The salt felt very smooth against the cold white chicken that night...'

An admirable attention to detail lies couched within that little speech, one whose perception is belied by the youthfulness of its creator. More importantly, Ridley Scott had finally shot his first film – and it was a promising one.

But *Boy* now went through an unintentionally prolonged post-production period. Scott had spent six weeks during the summer of 1961 shooting the film, before adding post-synced dialogue. He'd next shown the result to his teachers and classmates at the Theatre Design department of the Royal College of Art, where five other short films had also been made by the end of that year. Scott then warehoused *Boy on a Bicycle* after his graduation from the RCA, while he embarked upon a travelling scholarship to the United States. Two and a half years then went by.

During this period, Scott's former RCA mentor George Haslam had retired, and been replaced by Peter Newington, who came from Music and Arts at the BBC and had been involved with the British Film Institute.

Apparently, Peter was going through some old Theatre Design stuff when, one day in 1964, he came across *Boy and Bicycle* and had a look at it. Now, at that point the audio was very raw. But Newington must have seen something he liked because he got in touch with me and asked, 'Do you want to finish this properly?' I said, 'Sure!' So Newington got me a £250 grant from the BFI to mix the sound. I then spent some time in a tiny mixing theatre [with sound recordists Brian Hodgson and Murray Marshall] sweetening Tony's voice-overs. I also added some sound effects: seagulls, the tide coming in, street noises.

But then I had a problem. Originally I'd laid down a music track on *Boy and Bicycle* that had been composed by John Barry [*Out of Africa, The Ipcress File*, various James Bond films]. And even in the early Sixties Barry was quite a well-known and important musician. The cut was this little piece I adored called 'Onward, Christian Spacemen' [available as Track 21 of the 1993 Scamp compact disc collection, *John Barry: The EMI Years, Volume Three, 1962–1964*]. Now, I'd used that music because I'd never expected *Boy and Bicycle* to be seen commercially. But now that the British Film Institute was involved, such a thing was a real possibility. So I agonized over taking that music out. Then I just called up John Barry and said, 'Help me!' I was no one, of course, and he didn't know me at all. But I was honest with him and told Barry I'd done this little film and wanted to use 'Onward, Christian Spacemen' for it. But the price for music rights was expensive even in those days, and my film only cost me £65. So I told Barry I simply couldn't afford to pay him. Still, could he help me out?

John Barry was a very, very, very busy man, and always has been. But I think I somehow connected with him, because he told me to call him back. And I did that. For seven months! I kept calling and calling and he kept saying, 'Call me back, I'm busy now.' Then, probably in exasperation, with Barry thinking, 'Will this nightmare never go away?', he agreed to meet me. So I met John Barry in London. We had a drink and he said, 'I'll tell you what. I'll record a fresh version of "Onward, Christian Spacemen" on the end of a session I'm doing right now. I have a bit of the London Philharmonic there with me and I'll bash it off for you.'

Well, of course I was thrilled. The next Thursday I went down to this enormous music studio and watched Barry record the score for *King Rat* (1965, directed by Bryan Forbes). This was the first time I'd ever been in a real mixing room. I sat in the back, and didn't speak to anybody. Just watched Barry perform. Then, at the end of the recording – it was about ten o'clock at night – Barry asked the key artists to stay. He said, 'The rest of you guys can go. Thank you very much, everybody.' He then came round to me and said, 'Right, give me the tape.' I gave him a tape with the regular version of 'Onward, Christian Spacemen' on it. Barry went round to the front, played it once, and said, 'All right, you guys.' Then Barry raised his baton and conducted a compressed version of that tune. A short while later he handed me a new tape. And that's how John Barry came to record some music for my first film.

Scott's completed *Boy and Bicycle* (copyrighted 1965) was next screened by the BFI's Experimental Film Fund Presentation. Since it had been primarily funded by the British Film Institute, *Boy* then became the property of the BFI, which still owns it today. This situation (partially) explains why Ridley Scott's first film is not cur-

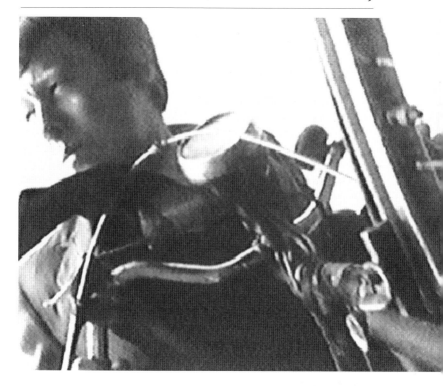

An example of the sophisticated imagery already on display in Ridley Scott's first film, the 1965 Boy and Bicycle **, starring the director's then 16-year old brother Tony Scott (pictured).**

rently available on video, since the British Film Institute has not yet chosen to release it in that format. It also explains why *Boy and Bicycle* is almost impossible to see.

Nonetheless, the arresting imagery, realistic treatment and relative technical sophistication of *Boy and Bicycle* were clear indications of the strengths marking many Ridley Scott films to come. Strengths that would be cultivated during the next phase of Scott's professional development.

2 Thirty Seconds of Perfection

After graduating from the Royal College of Art in 1961, Scott found himself facing a creative crossroads. On the one hand, he now had a degree in graphic design. On the other, he had been bitten by the film-making bug.

'By the time I was 19,' recalls Scott, 'I'd seriously begun thinking of becoming a film director, even though I was still drawn to advertising and set design. I didn't quite know *how* I'd become a director, but I figured I'd be one step closer if I could get a job designing sets at the BBC, because then I'd be working alongside directors. Which is exactly what happened.'

But not right away. Scott applied to the BBC for a post as a set designer in 1961, shortly after receiving his diploma from the RCA. He was then accepted for this position. However, at almost the same time, Scott won a travelling scholarship (in design) from another institution. This presented him with a dilemma – if he accepted his scholarship, he would not be able to join the BBC's ranks for another twelve months.

'Thankfully, the people at the Beeb were pretty understanding,' continues Scott. 'They told me they'd keep my position open for a while while I was travelling.'

Then, to use his own words, Scott 'immediately bolted to New York'. There he quickly landed a job with the Manhattan-based Bob Drew Associates, a top ad agency, where Scott experimented in photography and became a regular observer of the New York advertising scene. But Scott's tenure with Drew Associates was a brief one, as he explains:

I'd always fancied the fashion business, and since I'd also done a lot of still photography while I was at the Royal College – serious work, on big 20/16 rolls – I'd brought those pictures along with me to Manhattan, made them up into a portfolio, then used that to make contacts in the fashion world. I'd usually call up the secretary of whoever was running a big fashion house and say, 'Hello, I'm an English student. I'm in New York, I've got a portfolio, and I'm looking around for work. Can we set up an appointment?' And I'd get in every time. I'd sit and chat with these guys who were icons. They'd look slowly through my photographs and say, 'Mmmm, not bad. Maybe we can get something for you...'

So I did get a view into the super-glossy worlds of high fashion and advertising while I was in Manhattan. I really loved that. I remember being so impressed by the huge brownstones these guys had, how the walls of their businesses were covered with beautiful photographs. I thought 'My God, this is for me!' And I could have gone into one of those fashion businesses as an assistant, or a student intern. But then something else happened.

The 'something else' which lured Scott away from model runways and ad layouts was the realization that he'd focused on the wrong areas. 'When I first got to New York I thought I'd probably wind up with some kind of advertising job on Lexington Avenue,' Scott continues, 'which was then the hot place. But it dawned on me that I didn't really want to do that. Not to the exclusion of all else. Now, I'd always been in love with documentaries, and was a huge admirer of that kind of work, particularly the stuff [then] being done by Richard Leacock [co-director of *Primary*, 1960] and D.A. Pennebaker [also co-director of *Primary*, director of *Don't Look Back*, 1967, *The War Room*, 1993, and many others]. So I decided to drop advertising for a while and pursue the two best-known documentary film-makers of the time.'

Interestingly, Scott's youthful passion for documentaries would later inform, and become a key influence on, his own fictional work. For despite Ridley Scott's reputation as the quintessential cinematic stylist, he usually approaches character in his motion pictures by coaxing restrained, realistic, documentary-like performances from his actors. This results in non-stylized characters who are always convincingly human, no matter how fantastic their surroundings.

However, such influences would not reach fruition until after 1961, which is when Scott first approached Richard Leacock and D.A. Pennebaker, a meeting that resulted from a plan Scott had concocted with typically pragmatic aggression.

'I didn't know how to get to Pennebaker and Leacock,' Scott admits. 'But I knew where their offices [in New York] were, and I knew what Leacock looked like. And it's funny, but when you're on your own and you've got no one to ask and no one to help, you do all kinds of outrageous things. So one day I just stood around with my portfolio in the lobby of the building where these two guys worked, and in came Leacock with Pennebaker. They were headed for an elevator. So I shuffled in behind them, waited until the doors closed, and started my pitch. I introduced myself and quickly showed some photos and told them what I was about. By the time we got to the third floor, Leacock and Pennebaker were looking at each other, and I got a job.'

After resigning from Bob Drew Associates, Scott spent the remainder of his first trip to New York working in the editing rooms of Leacock/Pennebaker (who were employed by Time/Life Inc.). Among the documentaries on which he worked was one on Jawaharlal Nehru, the first Prime Minister of independent India, plus a documentary examining a college football game between Notre Dame and the University of Miami.

Scott recalls this last effort, in particular, as 'a real eye-opener. It took a look behind American student sport, and that was really stunning to an English person. I mean, at that time in Britain, you sort of reacted to sporting events with gentlemanly boos, you know? But I'll never forget how this one coach from the losing team acted in this documentary. His guys were in tears, crying in the dressing room, and this coach coldly said, "Well, because of how poorly you played, I guess God wasn't with us today." I was kind of gulping at that. I couldn't believe it!'

Scott spent eight months labouring on 'bits and ends' of such Leacock/Pennebaker efforts, all the while absorbing crucial lessons on how to edit films. Today he remembers this experience as crucial, educational and enjoyable. 'Leacock/Pennebaker was like the hot-shot production company of its day, because it was a melting pot for new talent. The guys working there were madmen. They'd do anything, shoot anything. My whole time there was just great.'

Still, despite his enjoyment, Scott-the-documentary-editor was constantly being reminded of a prior commitment he'd made as Scott-the-television-designer.

While I was at Leacock/Pennebaker, I was also getting letters from the BBC saying, 'We will hold your job open for another few months – how long before you come back?' And you know, if I hadn't had that job waiting for me in London, I probably would have settled in the States. But I did go back, eventually.

I had one last thing to do before I left America, though. While I was still in England, I'd been told by a student who'd done it before to go to Victoria Station and spend £70 ($100) on a special American travel ticket. This thing would then take me anywhere I wanted to go in the United States, up to 11,000 miles, on a Greyhound bus. So I wrote the BBC and told them I'd be taking another seven weeks of travel. Then I told Leacock and Pennebaker I was leaving, got on a Greyhound bus at 34th street in New York, and did this wonderful jog across America. New Orleans, El Paso, Las Vegas, Hollywood, Salt Lake City, Chicago and New York; that's where I sailed home to London.'

It was now 1962. On his return to England, Scott joined the BBC, where the next phase of his film-making education began.

'I was given a job immediately,' Scott says. 'And because I was a good designer, I didn't spend any down time working as an assistant. Instead, I was hired as a fully-fledged art director, to design sets for television.'

Scott then spent the next two and a half years at the BBC creating environments for everything from two-hour dramatic specials to weekly comedy series. 'I loved every minute of it, although at first, walking the tightrope between creativity and bureaucracy was very confusing. But what I discovered was that you learned how to beat the system. You learned how to get around estimates, for instance, or how to safely manoeuvre around fire regulations. Learning to be a designer also meant being forced to be fiscally pragmatic, understanding how to organize. Because at the BBC you had a thing called a budget. And if you went over that budget, you didn't have any more money. Period. But I really loved the battle of maximizing what you'd got – or what you hadn't got – in order to deliver for the director.'

Besides financial responsibility and on-set resourcefulness, the BBC also taught the young art director organizational methods and interdepartmental co-ordination techniques, seemingly mundane processes that were part of a larger underlying system allowing Scott's creations to move fluidly off the drawing boards and into the

BBC's construction division. There, Scott's sketches were turned into three-dimensional sets, ones that needed to be lit and shot in the most time-efficient manner.

'And I learned all that,' says Scott. 'In fact, the entire time I was at the BBC I was like the human sponge, soaking it all up. Being a designer there was, in a funny kind of way, almost like being a film director. You were always inside the nucleus of every project, working alongside the director and producer and lighting people and other department heads. And since you were really the boss of what the sets and props were going to look like, you were also sort of the *director* of those sets and props. So the BBC fundamentally taught me to know what I wanted. It also showed me how to communicate and organize with others, so that they could deliver what I wanted.'

While the aspiring film-maker had never been afraid of hard work in the past, Scott now found himself 'totally consumed' by his BBC position. Day after day, week after week, month after month, the young designer drew sets, detailed them, supervised their 'dressing', and immediately moved on to the next project. Such was Scott's total commitment, in fact, that he often made sure that certain sets he was working on contained a makeshift bed. This was done so that, after working throughout the day on a set, Scott could then spend the night there, literally sleeping on the stage floor before waking at first light to shower and clothe himself in a BBC dressing room. At which point he would begin the entire process over again.

By 1963, Ridley Scott's drive, talent and ceaseless energy (as well as a growing tendency to dig in his heels and fight for what he felt was creatively right), were beginning to be noticed within the grey halls of the BBC. These personal qualities brought Scott to the attention of certain other professionals outside the BBC as well. Among this latter group were a number of movers and shakers who would shortly enable Scott to combine his ingrained graphic talents with his newly acquired broadcast skills, all in the service of a newly emerging business arena called 'British commercials'.

A man who was very big at that time in English commercials was a director called Keith Hewitt, who I knew through my BBC contacts [Scott explains]. Keith used to do three commercials a week – he was on fire, that guy. And one day he said to me, 'Do you want to start [designing] commercials?' I said,

'Sure!' So Keith gave me four commercials to art direct, and the money I was paid for each of those was much more than what I was earning from the BBC. I thought, 'Jesus Christ! How long has this been going on?'

That's when I began to moonlight on the side by art directing commercials. I learned a lot from Keith during that period; he was an organized, pragmatic guy. Very creative, too. Now remember, at the same time, I was also working at the BBC. So sometimes I would draw a commercial set during the day, hand that off to Keith's builders, and then get on with my BBC set work. Then, that night, Keith's construction guys would put up my commercial set. I'd run over to their location at 5.45 a.m. the next morning to see it dressed, Keith would walk on to the set at 8.30 a.m. and tell me to bugger off, and then I'd dash back to the BBC in time to hit their 10 a.m. tea wagon. I did that for a year.

Despite what Scott now regards as his 'crazy' schedule, the young art director actually flourished under this system, adroitly juggling both his BBC and commercial responsibilities. So proficient did Scott become at this, in fact, that he was 'eventually asked to direct my own commercial. Of course I said yes. And the first commercial I directed was for Gerber's baby food. It showed a girl in a white leather coat and long white leather boots running down a tunnel. She was being pursued by some abstract fear. I stuck some music on that, like a rock video, and it all seemed to go over rather well. But the experience was really frightening; I had no idea of the chaos I was about to step into. That was the first time I'd experienced the conflict and the terror that happens when you actually move across the mark separating crew from director for the first time. I'd suddenly realized how important a director is. Because nothing, but nothing, will move without the director.'

In spite of his apprehensions, Scott's baby-food advert was generally perceived as a success.

What was more interesting in the long-term sense, however, was how Scott's first try as a (commercials) director gave him the opportunity to ignore a certain technical practice he'd long found rankling.

I used nothing but natural light on my first commercial. I wanted to make everything look real within the frame. That was exactly the opposite approach of the BBC at the time, where everything was lit very high-key and tended to look flat and unreal. That sort of lighting always pissed me off, because it made my sets look like shit. So I'd constantly be telling the BBC people that they didn't need all these bright lights blasting down.

In fact, one day I was on a stage that had been lit in the typical BBC way when a technician turned off an interior light to go to lunch. But he'd left on the exterior light that was coming through that set's window. And that exterior illumination gave the set's interior a very nice, very real, subdued look. So I asked the technician, 'Hey, why not leave it like this? It really looks good.' He told me, 'Can't, mate. It'll make the actors' faces go all dark.' I said, 'But that's what it looks like in real life! It's natural, like when you get home from work late in the day.' He replied, 'Nope. Sorry. It won't transmit. Nobody'll see anything.'

Well, I told him I thought that was bullshit. But I couldn't get anyone to listen to me, because this was basically a period when the technicians were controlling the process. However, sometime later, when I directed my first commercial, I did a low-key one, a natural-looking television commercial. And you know what? My lighting was dark and moody – and it transmitted just fine.

Unbeknown to the tyro film-maker, his insistence on natural sourcing and low-key illumination marked yet another crucial step forward in his aesthetic development, since he had unwittingly laid the foundation of what was to later become his signature lighting style. Yet this early triumph was undercut by an increasingly difficult schedule. Scott was now not only set designing for the BBC – he was also directing *and* designing commercials for other outside interests. And the round-the-clock effort needed to complete these assignments was placing an ever-increasing strain on both his professional and personal life.

Scott had married a fellow art student while enrolled at the RCA and, by 1963, he'd also acquired a brand-new house with a large mortgage. Adding to these stresses was the fact that this aspiring film-maker, who so desperately wanted to direct, had actually already been offered such an opportunity by the BBC. And had fumbled the chance.

By 1962, I'd only been art designing for about a year for the BBC. But during that year a position as a training director opened up at BBC2, and I applied for it. But I lost out on that one - blew the interviews, actually. I was going through a process I didn't yet understand. For instance, when I was first questioned about being a director, the interviewers started talking about theatre and about Shakespeare. The BBC was very formal then. I, on the other hand, didn't give two shits about this stuff. Since I tended to tell the truth, I told them: one, 'I don't really respond well to stodgy theatrical adaptations', and two, 'I'm very limited in my capacity to take in too much of Shakespeare.' Well, that was it for me, right? 'Get out!' they told me.

But the BBC finally did give me a director's course a year later. That was in 1963. And the director's course at the BBC was, as far as TV goes, probably as good as you could get. You were taken from your normal activities within that organization and put away for four or five months on a training programme. At the end of that period you then focused on your televised form of choice, be it an Ampex-taped play, a talk programme, drama, sports programme, interview show, whatever. Then you actually had to do one of these things under the BBC's time conditions. At which point everyone sat down and looked at each other's work and criticized it. Marvellous training, really.

Scott's televised form of choice was a dramatic half-hour recreation of a battle scene from Humphrey Cobb's novel, *Paths of Glory* (filmed by Stanley Kubrick, in 1957). To stage this fact-based, World War I story involving three innocent soldiers falling victim to the deadly politics instigated by their own officers, Scott designed the sets, wrote the script, tracked down the correct props (including vintage machine guns), and blocked out all the camera moves, which were then photographed with a borrowed 35mm motion picture camera. Scott also cast the lead of his own *Path* by personally obtaining the services of Keith Barron, a popular English television actor whom the director persuaded to give a *gratis* performance.

Ridley Scott's version of *Paths of Glory* was rehearsed for one full day, then photographed on the same night of that day in mid-1963. Although the end result was never intended for broadcast, Scott's *Paths* was deemed exceptionally praiseworthy by various students and instructors involved with the BBC's director's programme. Yet Scott himself mostly recalls his misgivings about the project.

'Doing my own *Paths of Glory* was a bit terrifying. Frankly, I wasn't sure that I'd nailed what I was after. Some of that hesitation, I think, came from the way I worked. I didn't like to explain everything, for example – I just did it, you know? I still don't like explaining everything. Anyway, at that point I wasn't very articulate, either. So I had very little feedback on *Paths*. It wasn't until after I'd asked for a telecine replay of what I'd shot, in fact, that I finally thought, "Whew – I've got a show!"'

Scott's short-form *Paths of Glory* also caught the attention of Tony Giles, a prominent BBC producer, who then contacted the neophyte film-maker with an offer to direct an episode of a new one-hour BBC television series. This was titled *Softly, Softly*, a police drama that had been spun off from another BBC TV series titled *Z-Cars*, itself an immensely popular police programme (one whose tone, content and cultural impact was similar to America's own late Fifties/early Sixties ABC-TV series, *The Naked City*).

Softly, Softly was scheduled to be broadcast 'live'. But according to Scott, being responsible for directing a live TV program wasn't nearly as daunting as figuring out how to prep that 60-minute programme.

One of the trickiest problems I faced with *Softly, Softly* was the short period of time I had to do it in. Between being asked 'Do you want to direct a TV show?' and getting that show on the air, I had exactly three weeks. Within the first ten days I was given an office and a secretary in the main BBC building, and had scripts and casting books left on my desk. Then I was told to get on with it. Somehow, I managed.

But I'll never forget what was going on while I was prepping my first programme. It was during the height of the Cuban missile crisis [October 1963]. I was sitting in the kitchen of my new house late one Friday night, drinking umpteen cups of coffee so I could catch my second wind and get back to the studio to set something up. And while I was sitting there, planning things in my head, I kept wondering which window the atomic blast was going to come through.

Scott needn't have worried. As had previously occurred with his short set-designing career and his even shorter-form *Paths of Glory*, Ridley Scott's directorial debut for *Softly, Softly* was considered a success. He then directed a handful of other *Softly* episodes, back-to-back. 'By now I was getting the hang of directing for television,' says Scott. 'I was applying all of my red tape knowledge from design to directing, and I'd started to realize there were similarities between the two. So I eased into broadcast directing fairly easily.'

Then, in early 1964, Scott was asked to work on another English television series. This one starred Ian Hendry (whom Scott thought 'a great actor' and who sadly subsequently died from alcohol abuse). The programme was *The Informer*.

That was a good series [recalls Scott]. It was also where I learned that television was not for me. I already was very frustrated with how television looked, and had started to play around with how the medium could be made better. And during my first shot at *The Informer*, I was reported on by a cameraman from that show. He told his higher-ups that I was always changing my mind. 'Well, that's my job,' I said. Apparently that didn't mean much, because I completed a one-on play [as part of *The Informer*], and then I was fired from the programme.

However, I'd already discovered that there was only so far you could go as a TV director, because there was only so far you could refine the process. I also discovered that I enjoyed editing and shooting inserts much more than I did overseeing this sort of lumbering process where you were talking from an electronic gallery down to six cameramen on the TV stage floor. So when somebody offered me the chance [early in 1964] to direct more commercials because of my background as a designer and director at the BBC, I jumped at it. And I quickly found that what I doing now was enough for me – I loved doing commercials. I loved turning footage, and loved the fact that commercials were on film. I loved how they were all visual. I loved the fact that I was dealing with beautiful pictures. To me, advertising films were little capsules of perfection. You also got an opportunity to craft a 30-second commercial much more often than you did a 60-minute television film.

Scott's jump from the secure harbor of the BBC into the treacherous waters of independent advertising actually proved a phenomenally successful career manoeuvre. For after only nine short months, during an intensely prolific period in which Scott mastered commercial techniques and began turning out one dazzling advertisement after another, his career underwent a radical upswing. A meteoric one, in fact, since Scott now quickly rose from a fired, ex-BBC employee to 'the biggest director in modern-day advertising'.

The preceding description, lifted from a British magazine of the day, is not an exaggeration. Although fellow countrymen/directors Alan Parker (*Midnight Express*) and Adrian Lyne (*Fatal Attraction*) had also begun to make their own impressive marks on the world of British TV marketing, it was Ridley Scott who was most often cited by his colleagues and the popular press as the ruler of this particular roost. His furious drive, fierce ambition and endless creative energy resulted in a veritable *tsunami* of slick yet cultivated work, scores of innovative commercials whose rapid-fire editing, striking compositions and sophisticated lighting techniques showed that Scott had not only fully absorbed the lessons then being taught by world-class directors like Richard Lester, Alain Resnais and Frederico Fellini, but that he was rapidly approaching their own level as a 'pure' film-maker.

Next came 1964. Ridley Scott was only 27 years old. He was also financially secure, influential, well-regarded and seemingly at the top of his game. Yet such were Scott's aspirations (and confidence) that he now informed the very production company through which he had achieved his recent triumphs – a company, Scott says, 'which really had been started up to service me' – that he would soon be *quitting* this company in order start his *own* business.

Scott's employers were first sceptical, then angry. 'Basically, they were in denial,' explains Scott. 'They kept saying, "You're not going to do this". I said, "Look, I've given you ten month's notice. I can't be any fairer than that. I know this is for me, and I'm going to do it. So start looking for another director."'

Ten months to the day after giving notice to his prior employers, Scott was painting the walls of his new office, which he'd leased at a location in London's arts-and-theatre-oriented West End. A few days later, that office opened its doors for business. It called itself Ridley Scott Associates.

RSA was started in late 1965. Scott hoped that this enterprise would be jumpstarted by his reputation as a gifted advertiser, and that a nurturing stream of old and new clients would soon come flowing into his firm. But Scott's reach almost exceeded his grasp.

'I sat waiting in my new office for almost a month,' Scott explains, 'and nobody came. Which wouldn't have been so bad if any money had been coming in, but it wasn't. In those days I was very foolhardy and confident. Instead of taking loans from somebody to start up RSA, I was living on the little bit I'd managed to save from my previous commercial work. And that was rapidly dwindling, since nobody was hiring me. Much later, I figured out why. I think my old clients were scared away because they knew from their own expe-

Scott loved his early career as a commercials director and produced several award winners, such as this one made in the early Seventies for Hovis bread. 'To me, advertising films were little capsules of perfection.'

rience that when you go out own your own for the first time, you're usually not solvent. So at first it looked like RSA was going to collapse. I watched my entire savings evaporate in four weeks.'

Then, towards the end of that four weeks, Ridley Scott Associates' saviour literally walked in through its doors. 'A guy from a big ad agency finally came in and said, "Would you care to design a commercial for us?"' Scott recalls. 'I casually said "Yes" [laughs]. That worked out, word got around, and suddenly, I was off again. But it was definitely touch and go there for a while.'

As RSA's workload began growing exponentially, Scott realized he could not personally handle every aspect of the increasing demand for its services. Therefore, he then began hiring other talented directors, producers and designers to work for the nascent company.

The first such person to be approached was Ridley's own brother, Tony Scott. The star of *Boy and Bicycle* had followed in his elder sibling's footsteps by recently graduating from the Royal College of Art; while there, he had expressed an interest in a career as a painter. But, like Ridley before him, Tony Scott had also evidenced a flair for film-making.

> While he was at the RCA, Tony had done two of the most confident student films I've ever seen. One was called *In Loving Memory*, and one was called *Missing*. Both were really good, and in a way far more ambitious than my own *Boy and Bicycle*. Tony had also been watching RSA doing really well, and us enjoying what we were doing, and I think Tony also liked the idea of the two of us doing films together. So since he'd recently left college, I kept after him to come join up with us – I told Tony my job at RSA was to elevate things. He finally came aboard, and I hired him as a designer. Then I taught Tony everything I knew about commercials and film-making, from the ground up. We'd always been close, so there wasn't any sibling rivalry involved. I just felt Tony was the best suited person I knew at the time to get the job done. He's certainly proven that a thousand times over since.

Indeed, Tony Scott soon became a valuable RSA associate in his own right, first as a designer, then as a director. Brother Ridley remained the RSA star, however, and within a few short years Scott was also hiring other promising film-makers to work for RSA. These included Hugh Hudson (*Chariots of Fire*), Peter Webb (*Give My Regards to Broad Street*) and several additional directors, all of whom initially cut their cinematic teeth directing commercials before moving on to feature films.

'At the time,' says Scott, 'I think RSA was one of the first firms really to get into the idea that a production company should have several in-house directors. But first I had to break down a lot of psychological barriers, since I was directing commercials myself. This is when I initially learned to function as a producer. Because whenever a new director was hired, I'd just back off, and strictly produce whatever it was they were directing. That way our new men would realize they weren't in competition with me, and that RSA was serious about letting them keep their own autonomy. Of course, this was also great for me, because I wound up learning how to produce. Anyway, RSA just kept building and building. It was very exciting, and very successful.'

Just how successful can be measured by the fact, that 34 years after its wobbly beginnings, Ridley Scott Associates boasts branch offices in London and Los Angeles and is still ranked among the world's best television and film commercial production companies. Much of that reputation stems from the early labours of Ridley Scott, who, through the late Sixties and early Seventies, continued to direct and/or produce an astonishingly prolific body of work – 3,000 RSA commercials, in fact, many of which were shot on location in England, America, France and other countries. Many of Scott's early commercials were also award winners; among his most acclaimed 'adverts' from this period were Scott-directed spots for the likes of Hovis Bread, Strongbow Cider and Levi Jeans.

The primary reason Scott's commercials were so well received was because of their increasingly daring visual sense. Besides the stylistic traits mentioned earlier, Scott's innovative approach was by now incorporating an unusual frontlit/backlit lighting scheme, heavily smoked sets, plus a comic-book-like sense of framing that mirrored the 'newspaper funny strips' he'd studied as a child. These preceding techniques, in particular, would attract much attention – and imitation – when Scott made his later transition to feature films.

'My influences and techniques, my style, if you will, really come from my education and by finding my own way through the commercial field,' adds Scott. 'I mean, I had seven years at two extremely progressive art schools to learn things like composition, and I picked up the functions of cameras and lenses and sound and performance by working on commercials. But if I were pressed to describe my style, to label it, I'd think I'd have to say it's called reality. Because no matter how stylized it gets, underneath it's real. That's where it works for me.'

3 First Attempts

The late Sixties and early Seventies were good years for Ridley Scott and RSA. Scott's company was growing by leaps and bounds, and so was his personal life: he had fathered two sons (Jason and Luke Scott) during this period.

'During the first decade of RSA we were doing really well and dealing with a lot of people responsible for injecting new blood into the popular culture – top fashion designers, painters, graphic designers, advertisers and musicians. Everyone at RSA was caught up in the "swinging London" scene, too,' Scott recalls, with a faintly bemused grin. 'We were all wearing pink velvet jackets and frilled shirts.'

Nevertheless, the film-maker still had not achieved his primary goal – to direct a full-length motion picture. This is why, in 1971, Scott began focusing on ways to realize that ambition.

'The reason I got out of commercials as my primary career was certainly not because of boredom – if anything, the dangerous thing about my first ten years doing adverts was how quickly the time passed,' Scott explains. 'Also, at the time I suddenly put my head up to take a breather, I realized how bad so many films were. Movies seemed to be going through one of their periodic "down" cycles, and since I was frustrated by what I was seeing in the theatres, I decided it was time to take the next logical step and go into movies myself.'

Scott also admits that a certain professional rivalry fuelled his decision: 'I was starting to go crazy because I was very frustrated about the fact that I had not yet done a film. And in a way, a real race was on between myself and my competitors, people like Alan

Parker and Adrian Lyne, who really were my main competition in advertising at the time. I knew them, and they were buddies, but Parker had already directed two low-budget movies. And I could see that RSA guys like Hugh Hudson and my own brother were also going places. This is when I seriously started to read possible film material. But after slogging through a lot of bad scripts, I was again inspired to sit down and write my own screenplay, which I hadn't done since *Boy and Bicycle*.'

Throughout 1971, Scott produced three self-penned drafts of a screenplay he entitled *Running in Place*. Envisioned as a low-budget 'heist' film, *Running*'s thriller aspects then attracted the attention of British performer Michael York, who expressed an interest in playing the lead. But after a year of development, the tentatively budgeted $1.2 million *Running in Place* abruptly stumbled over a budgetary shortfall and collapsed, just as the design process was getting under way. Scott was naturally frustrated; he was also characteristically unfazed by this setback.

'We'd gotten so close with *Running* that the project had involved a couple of Hollywood people,' Scott says. 'So I figured, well, at least now you're in the system. Some people in the industry now know who you are, and you can fly out to Los Angeles any time to catch the ear of the English community over there. The downside was that I'd realized that the way I'd gone about trying to write and develop *Running in Place* myself had been crazy – it was just too much work for a guy who was also running a business and shooting commercials full time. So I thought, why not just choose a subject and choose a writer and then have them do it? You could get a good writer in London for just five thousand pounds (eight thousand dollars) in those days.'

Following his own advice, Scott joined forces with screenwriter John Edwards in 1972 to co-create a script entitled *Castle X*. Described by Scott as ' a medieval horror film', *Castle X* attracted the attention of pop-music mogul Robert Stigwood, who'd recently added a film production arm to his parent company RSO (the Robert Stigwood Organization). RSO, in turn, bought Scott and Edwards' *Castle X* screenplay as a vehicle for Stigwood's enormously popular Australian singing group, The Bee Gees, whom Stigwood was trying to break into films. But after signing on as the director of *Castle X* and spending 'quite a lot of time' with the Bee

Gees, Scott was out of the country and scouting locations in Yugoslavia when Stigwood abruptly withdrew his financing from the film.

Like *Running in Place* before it, *Castle X* had collapsed just as it was starting up. Still undaunted, Scott moved forward by forming a creative alliance with a British playwright, author and screenwriter named Gerald Vaughan-Hughes. Scott had met Vaughan-Hughes through a mutual agent. And it was while discussing possible film projects with his new writing associate that Scott realized he and Vaughan-Hughes were both stimulated by the design possibilities inherent in historical pieces like *Castle X*. Therefore, the pair now concentrated their energies on creating screenplays which would not only be dramatically exciting but give full rein to Scott's art directing talents as well.

Two scripts resulted from this decision. The first was based on the Gunpowder Plot, a failed 17th-century conspiracy of English Roman Catholics, who planned to murder King James I, his queen and his oldest son by blowing up Parliament on 5 November 1605. Undertaken as a reprisal against James' increasing oppression of British Catholics, it was put into action by (among others) a British soldier named Guy Fawkes (whom Scott calls 'the first terrorist').

'Gerry then came up with another interesting idea,' Scott continues. 'He did a script on a mid-19th-century palaeontologist named "Indian" Capwell, who roamed around the American wilderness in places like Arizona with an old-fashioned camera, where local Indians showed him the remains of things they called big lizards. Of course, these were fossilized dinosaurs. Capwell was among the first people to photograph them, and Gerry's screenplay on the man was quite good. But when we tried to get it financed, the money people told us the project was a bit too intelligent.'

Scott may have been encountering difficulties launching his film career but, at the same time, his RSA firm was the most successful production company in London. It was his flair for commerce, in fact, which finally convinced Scott that the most expeditious way of starting his feature career would be by developing his own films in-house. Thus, in 1980, was born Percy Main.

Percy Main was the first production company Scott had begun for something *other* than commercials. Within a few months, the firm was choosing subjects, hiring writers, and developing scripts. Four years later, Scott expanded this business, established a location on London's Lexington Street, and renamed the firm Scott Free Enterprises.

'In a certain sense, I started Scott Free out of frustration,' reveals the director. 'I'd felt we were never going to get a movie made, so we should concentrate on getting our own dramatic material on to TV. With that in mind we hired a producer to run Scott Free named Steve Bailey, who was good, and who looked around for work for us in television that had nothing to do with commercials.'

One such opportunity arose from Technicinol, a French television company. Technicinol had recently had begun producing a series of classic literary adaptations (including the works of Henry James) for broadcast throughout France. Steve Bailey was aware of this programme, and persuaded Technicinol to allow Scott Free to contribute a segment. After all the necessary contracts had been exchanged, Technicinol then assigned Scott Free to adapt an 1885 Henry James story entitled 'The Author of Beltraffio'.

Ridley Scott was 'more than a little excited by this'. But his hopes of directing a prestigious literary adaptation were ultimately pushed aside by other factors.

My brother Tony had done a lot of commercials himself by now – this was 1975 – and he really wanted to direct something bigger too. So when the chance to do this French TV show came along, we both decided to leave the decision as to who would direct it up to fate. Basically, we tossed for it. And I lost. But Tony went ahead and did a good job on 'Beltraffio'.

Anyway, at that particular moment I was also reading a lot of classical literature which had fallen into the public domain – mainly so I wouldn't have to pay for it. And I discovered that I loved the work of Joseph Conrad. In fact, I wanted to get the rights to his *Heart of Darkness*, which I thought was a very ambitious novel. But after I'd investigated that I found Francis Ford Coppola had already either bought or optioned it with a view to making *Heart of Darkness* into a film. Which of course came out as *Apocalypse Now*. Next I discovered this Conrad short story entitled 'The Duel'.

'The Duel' was based on fact. Conrad had apparently been leafing through some newspapers and noticed a rather ironic acknowledgement of the death of a famous French Colonel, who'd served in the Napoleonic army. The article mentioned that this man had also actually duelled with a fellow officer over 18 times! So from that incident, Conrad had created this short story, which I really liked. But I think short stories frequently make the best kinds of movies anyway. Or certainly offer the best kind of basic plot line.

Scott now hatched the idea of turning 'The Duel' into a one-hour TV production. This proposal was presented to Technicinol, whose response was positive. Technicinol next put up a budget of £150,000 for Ridley Scott to direct 'The Duel' for French TV. But once Scott had chosen Gerald Vaughan-Hughes to adapt Conrad's short story into a screenplay – 'Gerry's an extremely good writer, and a great historian', Scott says – and after Vaughan-Hughes' final script had been delivered to Scott Free in 1975, what began as a short television programme started mushrooming into Ridley Scott's first feature film.

'Gerry's screenplay, which he'd called *The Duellists*, was a big, elegant thing. It was a lot better than anyone had expected,' continues Scott. 'And everyone sort of started to mutter about a feature. I then budgeted his script out as a film that would cost about $700,000. But at this point Technicinol graciously backed off – they just wanted to do TV – so I decided to position Gerry's script as something bigger than a 60-minute TV show.'

The Duellists opens in the year 1800, in Strasbourg, France, where a laconic Hussar named D'Hubert is asked to arrest a hot-headed fellow officer called Feraud, who has recently wounded the local mayor's nephew during a duel. Feraud takes immediate offence at D'Hubert's attempt to arrest him, and challenges the astonished D'Hubert to *another* duel. This takes place in an enclosed, claustrophobic garden. D'Hubert wins the match by knocking Feraud unconscious.

One year passes. D'Hubert and Feraud's paths cross again, and Feraud demands satisfaction for being 'humiliated'. This time D'Hubert is almost killed during the pair's second duel. Circumstances prevent Feraud from finishing the job, however, and for the next 15 years, as the Napoleonic Wars wage around them and both men rise to the rank of general, D'Hubert (who explains he keeps fighting as a matter of honour) and Feraud (who says he challenges D'Hubert to feed his sense of spite 'like a bloodsucking louse') continue their violent duelling, sometimes with pistols, sometimes with swords. By now D'Hubert is weary of Feraud's insistent attacks. But Feraud refuses to concede defeat, since none of their contests (thus far) has resulted in either man's death. Finally, it is 1816, the year of the men's last duel. This is played out in the deserted ruins of a crumbling castle, serving as a visual metaphor for the outmoded code of 'honor' which has brought the pair to this place. A nerve-racking game of cat and mouse now ensues, and leads to a surprising conclusion.

Despite its seemingly bare-bones storyline, Vaughan-Hughes' *Duellists* script was in fact admirably fleshed out with piquant dialogue, interesting observations on the social climate of its time, and included a thoroughly modernistic slant on the irrational conflicts between the rationalistic D'Hubert and brutish Feraud. Such were the merits of Vaughan-Hughes' screenplay that, following its polite dismissal by Technicinol, Scott decided to bring *The Duellists* to the attention of the then mighty British entertainment conglomerate EMI. However, EMI also turned down *The Duellists*. Rethinking his strategy, Scott next flew the script to Chicago, where he met with representatives from an American firm associated with the prestigious dramatic US television showcase, *The Hallmark Hall of Fame*.

At first, the *Hall of Fame* executives expressed an interest in transforming *The Duellists* into a major American made-for-TV movie. Unfortunately, the project's $700,000 budget ultimately proved 'too rich' for Hallmark's taste. 'But the head Hallmark man there actually gave me good advice,' Scott points out. 'He said, "You know, this is really a feature film. Why don't you try and make this into a movie?"'

Heartened by this reaction, Scott now called on an English production company named Enigma, which was being run by David Putnam, a then fledgeling producer who would later join the ranks of Britain's most distinguished film-makers. Putnam was impressed with Vaughan-Hughes' *Duellists* script; he then agreed to represent it as Scott's producer. Putnam next introduced Scott to David Picker, head of production at Paramount Pictures. 'And after a long, hard haul,' Scott continues, 'Paramount finally said they wanted to do *The Duellists*. This was in the fall of 1976. But nobody really took *The Duellists* seriously or accepted it, even after they'd greenlighted it. I think they looked on it as an unimportant, low-budget thing. I also had trouble being accepted as a developer and director, even though I thought Gerry's script was pretty bloody

Ridley Scott with David Putnum (left), during the shooting of Scott's first movie The Duellists**. Putnum agreed to act as producer after seeing Vaughan-Hughes' script. The budget for the film was so tight that Scott was forced to use Putnam and other crew members as extras.**

sophisticated and I already had a 10-year reel of commercials.'

Scott's apprehensions must have been justified during his initial budget talks with the studio, for the Paramount brass quickly made it clear that *The Duellists* was not exactly targeted as a prestige project.

One of the first things they haggled about was our budget [continues Scott]. By now that had grown to $900,000. But Paramount told us they weren't going to pour that kind of money into this kind of subject. David and I knew $900,000 was pretty low for a studio film, though, even then. So after a lot of discussions we finally got them to accept that amount. The way I cinched the deal was by telling Paramount that I would put up a completion bond for *The Duellists* (the guarantee that covers budget overages). I also told the studio, 'And by the way, we start pre-production today. And in a couple of months, we'll be shooting.' Well, their jaws just dropped. They said, 'But this is the fall! That means you'll have to start shooting in September! On location! You can't shoot a picture like this on location in the winter time!' I said, 'Yes I can. We do it now, or we don't do it.' I was afraid this thing would never happen if we waited until spring.

Well, taking that position was a good example of the reckless streak in me. I mean, I didn't fully understand completion bonds back then, and I sure as hell didn't realize what shooting some of *The Duellists* during winter was going to be like. We used a ski resort near Inverness in northern Scotland for a sequence in the film where the French army is bogged down by a winter on the Russian Steppes, for example, and it was bloody freezing! But if you've got to do something, you've got to do it.

Scott did, and Paramount agreed to his conditions – *The Duellists* was a 'go'. Casting became Scott's next priority. Paramount supplied him with a short list of performers whom they felt would help the project; at its top were Keith Carradine (who had recently impressed filmgoers worldwide with roles in Robert Altman's *Thieves Like Us* and *Nashville*), and Harvey Keitel (also on the rise following his appearances in films like *Mean Streets* and *Taxi Driver*). Scott was favourably familiar with both men's work and, after a short negotiation period, agreed to hire both of them. Not without opposition, however; at first, the Brooklyn-born Keitel resisted the idea of playing an 18th-century French officer, feeling he was 'all wrong' for the part. As Scott recalls. 'I then told Harvey that we also had an American from California and a bunch of Brits from London playing Frenchmen, so people really weren't going to get too upset with a New Yorker taking another one of these parts. The more important point, though, was this – I convinced Harvey that accents were the least of our troubles. Because if the story worked well, then within a couple of minutes the audience was going to get embroiled in the film and not notice accents anyway. Harvey saw the logic of that and we were off.'

Keitel was cast as the malevolent Feraud; Carradine as the more even-handed D'Hubert. Scott next began to contact various actors he had crossed paths with during his BBC and RSA years. Eventually, he assembled a remarkable roster of supporting per-formers for *The Duellists*. This group represented some of the best-known character actors in England: Edward Fox, Tom Conti, Pete Postlethwaite (here billed as 'Peter' Postlethwaite), Robert Stephens, Jenny Runacre and Diana Quick.

'Diana, who plays Carradine's mistress early in the film, was a particular help during casting,' adds Scott. 'She'd done a lot of great work with the Royal Shakespeare Company and, after we cast her, she came up to me one day and said, "You know, Albert Finney [*Tom Jones, Under the Volcano*] and I are mates. And Albert would probably love to do something in this. Let me speak to him." She did, and I will be eternally grateful to Albert for playing a small part in *The Duellists* (as Fouche) for a case of champagne.'

Scott also cast his two young sons, Jake and Luke Scott, in small parts. But now more practical matters loomed. After scouting loca-tions and breaking down its script, principal photography on *The Duellists* was scheduled to begin in late September 1976 (the film then wrapped production on Christmas Eve of the same year). Northern Scotland had already been chosen to stand in as the Russian Steppes; the film's primary shooting location, however, would be around the medieval town of Sarlat, in the Dordogne region of France, an unspoiled, Edenic area whose breathtaking pastoral landscapes provided ironic contrast to the violent human conflicts being played upon them.

'When I looked at some of the Sarlat locations, I couldn't believe them,' Scott says. 'Truly. They were so beautiful, it was like step-ping back in time.'

Yet *The Duellists* is suffused with qualities that elevate it far above simple admiration for a stunning use of natural landscapes. Its screenplay is subtle and mature, for example, and the production design is of the highest quality: the film's sets, props and costumes are astonishingly accurate, particularly for such a low-budget picture. Homes, beds, pipes, military uniforms, hairstyles, eating utensils – all seem to have been plucked from the past by some miraculous celluloid time machine and returned to our own century to service Scott's film.

This dramatic sophistication and visual verisimilitude was arrived at in a number of ways. 'First,' Scott begins, 'I was a designer… trained as a painter, and then as an art director, and from art direction I drifted into graphic design. And graphic design opens up all sorts of things, because it's photography, film and editing. So I had all that going in. I also had a couple of prior films in mind. The one I admired most at that point was Zinnemann's *A Man For All Seasons* (1966). You can see echoes of *Man* in *The Duellists* script, because *A Man For All Seasons* was very well written, and I thought we'd produced a pretty intelligent screenplay for *The Duellists* as well.'

When asked if *The Duellists* might also have been influenced by Stanley Kubrick's *Barry Lyndon*, itself a visually sumptuous production released in 1975, just one year before Scott's own feature began filming, the director laughs and says, 'Totally. I thought *Lyndon* was one of the most beautiful films I'd ever seen. At the time I'd also already done many commercials, and quite a few of them were period. I also was living in a 17th-century house that was essentially stone inside, like a castle in the Cotswolds. And I remember other little things, too, like watching how light functions with limestone.

'So all of this was brought to bear on *The Duellists*. It sounds pretentious, but I'm really an environmental Hoover (vacuum cleaner), sucking everything in. And I see beauty in everything. That sounds very "California", doesn't it? But that's how it is.'

Yet Scott's primary influences on *The Duellists* were cued into his abiding interests in painting and art. 'The best references on any period in history, of course, are its painters. So before we shot, I started to look at the Napoleonic painters and other artists. For instance, for my lighting effects I was studying guys like Georges de La Tour, who's actually way before that period [La Tour, a 17th-

century French painter, is justly famous for his candle-lit subjects].
Mostly, though, I studied artists who were great representational-
ists of that particular point in history.'

The Duellists' evocative opening shot certainly reflects this
approach, for it shows a young, white-bonneted peasant girl herd-
ing a gaggle of geese up a sun-dappled country lane. It is lit and
composed in such a way as to remind the viewer of some half-for-
gotten Dutch masterpiece. Was Scott's 'visual researching', then,
the impetus behind his decision to compose other key moments in
The Duellists as great works of art?

'Absolutely,' the director responds. 'My looking at so many paintings during pre-production definitely was the reason I adopted the
style of starting off some scenes – like that pull-back from the
cheese tray with the mice on it – as if they were still-lifes.'

Once Scott locked in the 'look' of *The Duellists* (a procedure
which also incorporated the use of rigorous storyboarding), he then
maintained its cinematographic design by acting as the film's primary camera operator. This practice of shooting his own motion
pictures, while unusual, was certainly nothing new to Scott. He had
already demonstrated great technical potential with his youthful
still photography, cementing that promise with his striking cinematography for *Boy and Bicycle*. Scott next began routinely photographing many of his commercials. Moreover, this habit of acting
as his own camera operator is a practice Ridley Scott continues to
exercise on most of his motion pictures (with the notable exception
of *Blade Runner*).

Acting as my own operator on *The Duellists* ran up against David Putnam's
theory, though [Scott says]. David kept saying a director shouldn't operate.
What precipitated this was an earlier incident. An operator we'd gotten for *The
Duellists* was on for the first few days and then got fed up. He said, 'I'm leaving, because you clearly know how to operate, and this isn't fun for me. So
you do it.' And I did. But Putnam was worried. He told me, 'Look, I'll give you
five days. At the end of five days, if we get behind schedule, we'll find an
operator.' I said, 'That's fine.' And what happened was, we ended up smack
on schedule. But there is a logic to a director operating his own camera, if
he's comfortable with it. Because a film director's camera is exactly like an
artist's pencil – it's their primary tool.

While Scott did indeed wind up shooting most of *The Duellists* (receiving an Operator credit for his work in the film's 'end rollers' in the process), this is not to suggest that he was also its Director of Photography, or DP. That responsibility fell to Frank Tidy. A British cinematographer, Tidy had previously collaborated with Scott on a number of earlier RSA commercials, but this was his first work as a fully-fledged feature DP.

A clutch of other *Duellists* crew members had also worked at RSA prior to their being hired for Scott's feature debut. Among this latter group were Dubbing Editor Terry Rawlings, Focus Puller Adrian Biddle, and Associate Producer Ivor Powell (some necessary words of clarification here: an associate producer is actually the British equivalent of a US line producer – someone who handles the day-to-day producing chores of a motion picture during its principal photography phase). Each of these men would subsequently form part of an unofficial 'Ridley Scott support group', one that Scott would periodically utilize for later films. Ivor Powell, for example (nephew of acclaimed British film critic Dilys Powell), would line-produce both *Alien* and *Blade Runner*, while Terry Rawlings became principal film editor for *Alien*, *Blade Runner* and *Legend*. Adrian Biddle, of course, is now a distinguished cinematographer – but first he served as a DP for Scott's *Thelma and Louise* and *1492: Conquest of Paradise*.

Three final *Duellists* crew members should also be mentioned. Production Designer Peter Hampton and Costume Designer Tom Rand, in particular, did much to translate Scott's general concepts into a meticulous array of early 18th-century sets, props and wardrobe, each a shining tile in an overarching mural dedicated to the thoroughly convincing recreation of a bygone era. And Fight Director William Hobbs (who also coached sword-fighting sequences for such disparate films as *The Empire Strikes Back* and *Captain Kronos, Vampire Hunter*) had perhaps the most high-profile job on Scott's first feature. For it was Hobbs' responsibility to rehearse, block out and direct the half-dozen sword and pistol duels which dominate the film.

'Hobbs was a master swordsman,' recalls Scott. 'He was particularly good at teaching Keith and Harvey the finer points of handling rapiers and flintlocks, which they sometimes had to use on horseback in the film. Hobbs was also great at finding dynamic ways to stage their duels for the camera.'

With such a talented cast and crew at his disposal, the actual experience of making his first full-length film was, as Scott now recalls, 'smooth and enjoyable', despite such obstacles as a tight shooting schedule and minuscule budget. The latter not only forced Scott to use producer David Putnam and a number of other *Duellists* crew members as extras during a major cavalry charge, but forced the wardrobe department to wrap them in purloined hotel blankets for the scene, because the production could not afford the cost of dressing these dragooned crew members in extra uniforms.

By mid-1977, post-production concluded on *The Duellists*. 'Once we'd shot and edited and scored what we'd done, Paramount was a little bit surprised at its quality,' continues Scott. 'Studio people didn't really pay attention to low-budget films in those days; no one from Paramount, in effect, turned up on the set when I was filming *The Duellists*. I thought they'd forgotten about me. But when I got back to LA with the final product, David Picker and Michael Eisner and Barry Diller, who were also at Paramount then, all saw it and loved it.'

With good reason. *The Duellists* is a remarkably assured debut, technically dazzling, thematically mature,with a dark, melancholy, densely textured ambience unexpectedly punctuated by frenzied battle scenes and viscerally staged sword fights. All in all, Scott had created a handsome production with that serious edge so characteristic of a quality British literary adaptation, the kind for which the English are justifiably famous. Which makes the relative obscurity into which *The Duellists* soon fell all the more puzzling. Once available on Paramount Home Video, virtually forgotten today, only occasionally revived on American cable TV channels like American Movie Classics and Bravo, *The Duellists* has seemingly slipped through the pop culture cracks – it remains Ridley Scott's least-seen, least-appreciated work. One wonders how long this distressing state of affairs will continue, however, since this is definitely a film ripe for rediscovery.

In any event, *The Duellists* had no problem being recognized as a quality product at the time of its initial release. Scott's debut feature won the Special Jury Prize at the 1977 Cannes film festival; it then went on to earn rave reviews from discerning critics on both

Keith Carradine and Harvey Keitel in The Duellists. **Visually stunning, Scott was influenced by the late Stanley Kubrick's lavish** Barry Lyndon, **which had been released just one year before Scott started filming. Scott thought** Barry Lyndon **'one of the most beautiful films I'd ever seen'.**

sides of the Atlantic. The rewards which *The Duellists* bestowed upon its director, however, were of a more personal nature.

When asked what Scott feels he'd best accomplished with his first feature film, the director thinks for a moment, then replies: 'I thought I'd handled the process. That's it. Which sounds like a simple answer, or a silly one. But just being able to get through the procedure and deliver a reasonably workable film was very reassuring to me. It wasn't until I'd really done my first feature that I found out how tricky making a feature is. And while I was making *The Duellists*, I was always in doubt. About telling a full story, and filling the two-hour slot. About pacing the actors and pacing the characters. I was particularly surprised about finding out what music does for you, and how you can expand areas of film that you never thought you could with the right soundtrack. So when all of that came together, it was pretty encouraging, you know?'

Scott was not pleased, however, with the manner in which *The Duellists* was distributed to American theatres in 1978 – or, rather, not distributed. 'I wasn't at all happy with its release,' Scott says. 'Paramount only gave me seven prints of *The Duellists*. In fact, during its initial run the film only played in one theatre in all of Los Angeles. That was the Fine Arts, on Wilshire Boulevard. Another of the problems was that it was misunderstood. Contrary to what many thought and how the critics approached it, *The Duellists* was not an art film. In fact, while I was shooting, I had thought of it in terms of a western. Yet it was booked on the art-house circuit. Consequently, *The Duellists* never reached the large-scale audience it was intended for.'

No matter. The larger issue – that Scott had finally directed his first motion picture – had been conclusively resolved to his general satisfaction. That this tyro effort had also been released by a major studio, and accomplished at an age when most other people would never dream of leaping into a brand-new career (Scott turned 40 while working on *The Duellists*), only sweetened the sense of accomplishment.

Besides, Ridley Scott's next project would most definitely snare the large-scale audience he'd missed capturing the first time around.

4 The Beast

With a first feature in the can, it was inevitable, given his boundless energy and restless creativity, that Ridley Scott would quickly begin assessing material for his second motion picture.

One potential project was the story of *Tristan and Isolde*. These were the principal characters of a medieval romance/adventure poem (itself based on ancient Celtic legend) whose archetypal original has not survived. Since the 12th century, however, Tristan and Isolde (or 'Iseult') has been retold in many forms, with echoes of their tale found in the King Arthur legend as well as *Romeo and Juliet*. *T & I*'s central plot has the young, heroic Tristan venturing to Ireland to ask for the hand of the Princess Isolde for his uncle, King Mark of Cornwall. He succeeds in this, but on their homeward journey Tristan and Isolde accidently drink a love potion originally meant for the Princess and the King. Henceforward, Tristan and Isolde are bound to each other by an imperishable love that does not destroy their loyalty to King Mark – who, enraged, separates the young lovers before their eventual tragic deaths.

Scott first began seriously considering *Tristan and Isolde* while on location for *The Duellists*. 'When we were in France, and looking at everything around us in the Dordogne, I thought, "My God, this is a romantic place. In fact, it's the perfect place to be thinking about a subject like Tristan and Isolde,"' the director says. 'So I talked to David Putnam about making *Tristan* my next film, and Gerry Vaughan-Hughes prepared a *Tristan* screenplay for us.'

Vaughan-Hughes' script was presented to Paramount, which put the project into development in the spring of 1977. Scott next began shuttling between London (where he still ran RSA) and Los

Angeles, where producer Putnam set up a Tristan production office. At the same time, long-time RSA collaborator and *Duellists* Associate Producer Ivor Powell helped co-ordinate the evolving project from England.

Earlier, Powell had also introduced Scott to a certain publication which would profoundly influence the director's next three films. 'I've always been a science fiction buff,' explains Powell, '[and] I also enjoy comic books – good ones, like *Heavy Metal*, which was being published in France under the title *Metal Hurlant* while we were prepping *Tristan and Isolde*. *Heavy Metal* is sort of a graphic arts magazine for adults, and in 1977, it was featuring a tremendous roster of artists. People like Jean Giraud, or Moebius, as he calls himself. Moebius always designs everything from the ground up in his science fiction stories. Wardrobes, buildings, weapons, transportation systems, everything. So, since I knew Ridley was interested in all types of art, I felt he'd probably like this, too. That's why I showed him a copy of *Heavy Metal* when we were in the Dordogne doing *The Duellists*. Ridley apparently hadn't been aware of the magazine before [this]. But [he] took one look at [*Heavy Metal*] and said something like, "Bloody hell! Why don't they make films like this?"'

Finding himself 'deeply affected' by *Heavy Metal* – particularly issues featuring 'Arzak', a Moebius-created character inhabiting a partly futuristic, partly medieval world – Scott omnivorously devoured past issues of the publication while experimenting with ways the approach of certain *Heavy Metal* artists might be reflected in his own films. One was to graft a *Metal* aesthetic on to *Tristan and Isolde*'s production designs. According to the director, '*Heavy Metal*, like *Kubrick's 2001*, which I thought was brilliant, made me realize how the environment of a fantasy or science fiction piece could be raised to a much higher level. That insight made me aim for a very exotic, "no time, no place" look for *Tristan*. Something that was historical, but in a gritty, stylized, *Heavy Metal* kind of way. Where the heroes would more closely resemble down-on-their-luck cowboys than traditional knights in shining armour.'

By mid-1977, *Tristan* storyboards and a revised draft of Gerald Vaughan-Hughes' script had been completed. 'And then I was completely waylaid by another film that came out in the summer of 1977,' Scott continues. 'I was in Hollywood at the time. David

Putnam said to me, "Why don't we go see this new film? I understand it's pretty good." So we trooped down to Mann's Chinese
Theater and saw this thing called *Star Wars*. And I was devastated.
Devastated because George Lucas, in some respects, had already
taken the same design paths I was planning for *Tristan and Isolde*.
I also realized while watching *Star Wars* that the *kind* of picture I
was trying to do with *Tristan*, this medieval love story, was never
going to find any real sort of audience. So while I liked and
admired Lucas's picture, the general experience of seeing *Star
Wars* was actually sort of depressing to me."

Unbeknown to Scott, the London-based head of 20th Century
Fox's UK division, Sandy Leiberson, had also recently seen a film
he could not shake. This had been *The Duellists*, which Leiberson
had caught during a Cannes Film Festival screening. Impressed by
Scott's talent, Leiberson next flew to Los Angeles, where he
searched through a number of projects in development at Fox in the
hope of discovering something Scott would find attractive.

One such property was a tense, terse screenplay titled *Alien*. It
began with the crew of a futuristic spacecraft tracking a mysterious
distress call to a forbidding 'planetoid', where they discover a
bizarre derelict spaceship and an ancient alien pyramid (later
dropped from the script). The pyramid houses large, leathery
'eggs'; one of these disgorges a small organism, which securely
clamps itself around a crew member's face and causes him instantly to lapse into unconsciousness. Once the human explorers have
brought their stricken comrade back to their ship and blasted off
from the planetoid, however, the clinging 'Facehugger' dies, leaving its victim seemingly unharmed. But the creature has actually
secreted an alien parasite within the man's body. This rapidly
growing organism viciously claws its way out of its 'host's' chest,
scampers away into the darkest recesses of the ship, and quickly
grows to the size of a human adult. It then picks off the hapless
humans, who cannot discover a way to stop it, until the creature is
finally killed by Ripley, a woman who is the ship's last surviving
crew member.

Obviously, Leiberson had uncovered a story whose narrative
skeleton had, in various incarnations, fuelled countless low-budget
genre pieces. But Leiberson saw something else in *Alien*'s leanly
executed script. For one, it had been co-written by Walter (*48*

Hours) Hill, already a respected screenwriter/director. The *Alien* screenplay also evidenced a certain power, maturity and cynicism rare for most science fiction projects. Leiberson therefore took the *Alien* script back with him to London, before forwarding it on to Ridley Scott in early 1978.

Alien's 'backstory' comprised more than a stripped-down script, however. The screenplay had originally been written (under the title *Star Beast*) by Dan O'Bannon, a then aspiring, recently unemployed scenarist. O'Bannon had been part of an aborted attempt by Chilean director Alejandro Jodorowsky (*El Topo, Santa Sangre*) to film a French-financed adaptation of the classic science fiction novel *Dune*. After *Dune*'s collapse, O'Bannon had hooked up with aspiring producer Ron Shusett. Both men then generated *Star Beast* as a low-budget project for O'Bannon to direct and Shusett to produce. But after some rewrites (and a title change to *Alien*), O'Bannon's screenplay was optioned by a new, Fox-associated development company named Brandywine Productions.

Brandywine co-founders Walter Hill, writer/director David Giler (*Fun with Dick and Jane*), and producer Gordon Carroll (*Pat Garrett and Billy the Kid*) had been excited by *Alien*'s commercial possibilities, sensing O'Bannon's screenplay would make a popular '*Jaws* in space'. Giler and Hill then rewrote O'Bannon's effort, leaving the original author's story outline and sequence of events intact but completely altering the script's dialogue. Giler and Hill also added numerous other refinements, including switching the gender of *Alien*'s protagonist (Ripley) from a man to a woman. This composite screenplay was the one which eventually landed on Ridley Scott's desk.

Sandy Leiberson, who was an important guy at Fox, was the first one to send me the *Alien* script [Scott continues]. Since that meant he took it seriously, I read it right away. But while I was intrigued by Leiberson's willingness to invite me to the Hollywood dance, a dance I was quite willing to participate in, I was also somewhat baffled, because my knowledge of science fiction at that point was barely minimal. I mean, I certainly had never made one of these pictures. In fact, I'd only seen a handful of them – *The Day the Earth Stood Still, 2001, Star Wars*. And as a rule, other than the ones I just mentioned, I didn't really like science fiction pictures. They seemed pretty silly to me.

But Leiberson thought I might be able to bring something different to a sci-fi. And once I started reading *Alien*, I was immediately hooked, right from the first page; it sort of sucked you in and never let you poke your head up. Beyond the way it was written, I was impressed with the script's vividness, the way things kept leaping off the page into my mind's eye. I also responded to a subplot concerning the owners of the human spacecraft, which was this sinister, Big Brother type of corporation, and I was quite taken with the then somewhat novel concept of the hero being a woman. [But] the thing that really appealed to me most about *Alien* was its characters. I really liked them, and they were clearly defined. Everything you needed to know about these people was beautifully set up within the context of the story itself, [which] included an interesting social subtext emphasizing the class differences between the command officers and the guys sweating it out on the engineering decks.

Excited by *Alien*'s design possibilities, sympathetic to its characters, Scott let Leiberson know he was interested in directing the project for Fox. The English film-maker then asked Paramount to be released from *Tristan and Isolde*, which Scott felt 'had lost its momentum'. Simultaneously, Leiberson contacted Alan Ladd Jr, Fox's Los Angeles-based Production Chief, with Scott's offer to direct *Alien*. Ladd had already greenlighted *Alien* as a 'go' project on Halloween Day, 1977, when Walter Hill had shown an interest in directing the film. But Hill had subsequently moved on to other projects, so Ridley Scott was signed as *Alien*'s director in February 1978 instead.

David Giler, Walter Hill and Gordon Carroll were contracted as the film's producers (although only Carroll and Ivor Powell would actually produce on a day-to-basis while *Alien* was involved in principal photography). The film's shooting was targeted to begin on 3 July 1978 and end on 21 October; 17 additional days for various inserts, pick-ups and reshoots were later accomplished during November and December. As for budget, Fox originally priced *Alien* at a meagre $4.2 million. Scott felt this sum unrealistic, however, and after storyboarding the entire film himself, the director presented his boards to the studio as a way of illustrating the elaborate visual scheme he intended to apply to the film. Fox then doubled *Alien*'s budget to approximately $8.5 million.

On the advice of Dan O'Bannon (who, along with Shusett, was still attached to the project), Scott screened *The Texas Chainsaw Massacre* to familiarize himself with state-of-the-art cinematic horror. He also repeatedly watched *The Exorcist*, a film Scott greatly admired, not only 'for the way it portrayed absolute evil, but because of the classy way it presented that evil'. Scott then put on his production designer hat to determine *Alien*'s 'look'.

'I stepped into *Alien*, in a way, almost by accident,' Scott says. 'I hadn't or would never set out to do that kind of movie, really. But when the script was sent to me, I had been burying myself in the area of *Heavy Metal* comics and graphic novels and other similar things, and *Alien* seemed well suited for those types of design possibilities. In fact, *Alien* really was the first film I did with a *Heavy Metal* sensibility. I think that's pretty obvious to anyone who saw the film and is also familiar with the magazine.'

Alien's comic-book roots had already been stimulated by Ron Cobb, an established political cartoonist and budding film designer who had previously created several creatures for the 'Cantina Sequence' in *Star Wars*. Cobb had been hired by O'Bannon for *Alien* design work before Scott's arrival, after which the English director retained the American artist and assigned Cobb the task of designing *Alien*'s human spacecraft, the mechanisms within it, and almost everything else connected with the Earthian culture portrayed in the film. The human spacesuits and wardrobe, however, were, at Scott's insistence, specifically designed by Moebius, the same French artist he had been so taken with during his first exposure to *Metal Hurlant*. Also hired for *Alien*'s nascent art department was RSA alumnus Michael Seymour, an Englishman who had worked alongside Scott on many commercials and helped integrate the efforts of Scott, Cobb and Moebius into a united visual scheme as the film's Production Designer.

The preceding employments still left Scott with one key *Alien* graphic question unanswered, however. Who would design the film's titled *Alien*, plus the three separate life-stages its goes through as it transforms into an adult?

The hardest part about making any 'Beast' movie [says Scott today], is deciding what the fucking Beast is going to look like. I knew I was in dangerous waters regarding *Alien*'s creature from the start, because almost all of the 'monsters' I'd seen in other films were pretty tatty. Therefore, I had to find someone capable of taking our own Beast up to the next level. That's where H.R. Giger came in. Giger is an excellent Swiss painter and sculptor, a surrealist, really, who's very technically accomplished but also drawn to grotesque imagery. Giger invented this remarkable style he calls 'biomechanics', which combines organic life with machinery. Anyway, after Dan O'Bannon gave me a book of Giger's art one day [*Giger's Necronomicon*] I started flipping through it and nearly fell off my desk. Because I'd lit upon a particular painting with this frightening, truly unique creature in it. I took one look at the thing and said, 'Good Christ! This is it! This is our Beast!' That was that. I'd never been so sure of anything in my life.

The painting Scott is referring to was entitled 'Necronom IV'. In it was featured a half-human, half-reptile creature with a fantastically elongated cranium. This long, loaf-like skull resembled nothing less than a gigantic grey penis. Such a resemblance was not coincidental, since Giger often used suggestive sexual imagery in his art. What is remarkable was how Ridley Scott would elaborate upon this penile token and enlarge it into a running *Alien* motif. For example, the small, crustacean/spider-like 'Facehugger' would be equipped with a pair of outsized, blatantly testicular lungs; the huge ovoid portals by which the film's astronauts enter the derelict spacecraft look like 15-foot-high vaginas. *Alien*'s sexual symbolism percolates throughout the metaphoric level as well, since the initial Facehugger creature 'fertilizes' its host through an aggressive oral rape while the larger adult dispatches its prey by thrusting a long, rigid, tooth-encrusted, obviously phallic tongue into its victims' brainpans, literally killing them by an act of penetration.

In any event, under Scott's urging, H. R. Giger was hired by Brandywine not only to design *Alien*'s adult creature and its Egg, 'Facehugger' and 'Chestburster' incarnations, but to create the look of the planetoid surface and the film's otherworldly, totally non-human derelict spacecraft. The artist ultimately spent months on the film, even working inside a special soundstage workshop on the Shepperton Studio lot (the English facility where *Alien* was filmed) in order to construct a life-size sculpture of the full-size *Alien* 'suit' later worn by wiry British stuntman Eddie Powell and six-foot, ten-inch tall Nigerian art student Bolaji Badejo, both of whom portrayed the menacing creature in the film. 'People sometimes talk about how Giger moulded a real human skull into his full-scale *Alien* sculpture as an example of how frightening his stuff is,' Scott says. 'What I think that observation misses is because Giger used real human and animal bones throughout the film, such materials added to the realism of what he did. What I find most frightening about Giger's work is the extra quality of reality he brings to his dark fantasies. It's the realism that makes Giger's work so strong, not the fantasy.'

Other key positions on *Alien*'s staff included Director of Photography Derek Van Lint (yet another RSA associate, whose work on *Alien* would constitute his sole credit as the Director of Photography on a feature film), Editor Terry Rawlings, Special Effects Supervisors Brian Johnson and Nick Allder (who handled the film's various miniature spacecraft, planets and model sets), and Associate Producer Ivor Powell. At one point Scott also thought of using a synthesized version of Holst's *The Planets* (composed by Japanese New Age musician Tomita) to score *Alien*, but ultimately reconsidered and hired respected film composer Jerry Goldsmith instead.

'Jerry did a very successful score for me for *Alien*,' Scott emphatically points out. 'I mean, it was absolutely brilliant. Spooky but beautiful. I still hear it today. The cue where the lights come up in the hypersleep chamber, for instance, or the music for that shot when the [human spacecraft] has separated from the refinery it's towing and yaws to port – the cues for those moments still send shivers down my spine. Even today, when I see films where the music is desperately trying to be scary in a certain kind of way, I think, "Ahhhhh, *Alien* !"'

Despite his endorsement of Goldsmith's efforts, however, Scott was not totally pleased with all of the composer's *Alien* music. In conjunction with editor Terry Rawlings (who typically attaches his own tempo music tracks to the films he is cutting), *Alien*'s director substituted certain cues scored for *Alien* with ones Goldsmith composed years earlier for John Huston's *Freud* (1961). Scott and Rawlings also replaced the end-credits music Goldsmith wrote for *Alien* with a movement from classical composer Howard Hanson's *Symphony No. 2, 'Romantic'*. This substitution, at least in this writer's eyes, was actually an improvement over Goldsmith's original end-credits score. For Hanson's music – wistful, sweet, 'feminine'– lends *Alien*'s ending a hard-won but peacefully triumphant note, whereas Goldsmith's original end-credits score – a recapitulation of *Alien*'s Gothic/action cues – would have closed the film conventionally by recycling music already associated in the audience's mind with terror and/or excitement.

Once *Alien* began production, Scott threw himself completely into all aspects of the film. For instance, the name of the Earthmen's spaceship had already gone through a number of changes before Scott appeared, from the *Snark* to the *Leviathan*. Scott, reaching back to his experience with *The Duellists* and the works of Joseph Conrad, suggested that the ship be renamed the *Nostromo* after a Conrad novel. Other Conradian references also seeped into *Alien* via Scott. The *Nostromo*'s shuttlecraft, for instance (the *Narcissus*), was named after Conrad's *Nigger of the Narcissus* (a work which, not coincidentally, involved a ship's crewman infected with a deadly disease). It was also Scott who came up with the idea of referring to the venal 'Weylan-Yutani' corporation which owns the *Nostromo* in the film as 'The Company', the same name as that of the organization whose riverboat sailed into Conrad's *Heart of Darkness*.

Casting was another key area of involvement by Scott. Rather than rely on the usual 'B' actors so common to low-budget science fiction films, Scott decided instead to move *Alien*'s performances 'up to the next level' by assembling an ensemble of evocative American character actors – Tom Skerritt, Harry Dean Stanton and Yaphet Kotto – and substantive British film/television/theatre stars like Ian Holm and John Hurt (who replaced British Shakespearean/film actor Jon Finch in the role of Kane shortly after shooting began). Scott's casting choice for Ripley, however, was his most audacious stroke. A tall, 28-year-old, virtually unknown New York stage performer named Sigourney Weaver – whose previous film work was restricted to two bit parts – was picked by Scott to portray *Alien*'s tough-minded protagonist, 'primarily', Scott adds, 'because of Sigourney's own strength and intelligence'.

Scott had no problems rounding up his cast, he explains, because of *Alien*'s script and sets, which included maze-like, claustrophobically enclosed, fully functional compartments for the *Nostromo* and an enormous derelict ship control room sporting a fossilized, elephant-like, extra-terrestrial pilot nicknamed 'the Space Jockey'.

The Swiss painter H. R. Giger visualized, and helped to design, the Alien creature. The artist used human and animal bones in the production of the beast, including a real human skull, helping to create a realistically menacing presence. The film won an Academy Award for Best Special Effects.

One of the reasons I've always felt it important to totally create the environment in a film is because the environment is a proscenium in which your actors perform, whether that proscenium is period or futuristic or contemporary. I believe the better the environment, the better your actors will respond. Part of this attitude is the designer in me coming out, of course. But if you were an actor walking on to a set like *Alien*, all you had to do was take a quick look around to know that we were serious about this motion picture, that we were not playing at games with science fiction. And I think one of the reasons I bagged such a good cast for *Alien* was that I could show them Giger and Ron Cobb's stuff and say, 'These are the trappings that will support our script.' In any event, I did feel that designing the environment inside *Alien*'s crafts was almost as interesting an exercise for me as getting its story right.

Scott again acted as his principal camera operator on his second motion picture, with the director today estimating that he shot 'approximately 80 per cent of *Alien*' himself. However, although the film would eventually be lauded not only for its photography but for its ground-breaking sets, eerie production designs and state-of-the-art creatures (surely the main reason *Alien* later received an Academy Award for Best Special Effects), the *personal* toll taken on the motion picture cast and crew was high.

Brandywine (and the Fox brass) maintained iron control over expenditures during production, and *Alien*'s director often felt economically constrained by 'not being able to go the little extra yard that would have fully delivered what we were trying to put on the screen.' Scott was also not satisfied with the film's miniature/special effects photography, which had almost been concluded by the end of principal photography. Therefore, Scott ordered this footage scrapped and, under his own supervision, totally reshot *Alien*'s model effects during post-production. Many *Alien* crew members also found themselves working 18-hour days, six to seven days a week.

Perhaps *Alien*'s most stressful aspect was the strained atmosphere on the shooting floor. This has been described to this writer by various participants in the film as 'tense' and 'uncomfortable'. The performers had split into separate camps, Sigourney Weaver felt particularly isolated, and Scott himself was viewed as intense and remote. Yet today *Alien*'s director can look back philosophically on what he felt made making *Alien* an uncomfortable experience.

I think the director generates the energy on a set, and on *Alien*, the energy coming from me wasn't comfortable [Scott explains candidly]. I was twitching like crazy, frankly because I was nervous. This was my first Hollywood picture. I was also frustrated because, for the first time in my professional career, there were hands other than my own on the film. And I'd never, ever been in this type of hands-on situation in my life. You've got to remember that one. At the time I made *Alien*, I'd already made my own world. I was a wealthy young man literally driving a goddamn Rolls-Royce. In fact, I remember Sigourney one day in the car park. She walked past me as I was getting out of my Rolls and said, 'Where did you get that? From your dad?'

'What could I tell her? I'd already been running my own successful business for over ten years at that point, but nobody seemed to recognize how far I'd come. I had also never had anybody question everything I did before *Alien*. I was repeatedly called on to justify my every move, whereas my natural inclination is to say, 'I know what I'm doing. Just let me get on with it, all right?' So the tension on the *Alien* set, I think, was partly due to my own insecurity and partly because I was being asked what, in my opinion, were so many stupid questions. And of course I was not able to say, 'Look, relax. Just trust me and we'll get it.' So yeah. On *Alien*, you could say there was tension.

This pressure increased shortly before the film's release, when Dan O'Bannon fought a bitter Writer's Guild arbitration battle with Giler and Hill over who should receive final credit for *Alien*'s script (O'Bannon, as it transpired, although many of those close to the production insist that Giler and Hill's screenplay contributions were substantive, and only uncredited because of a WGA technicality).

Despite the pains associated with its growth, however, *Alien* proved an incredibly popular motion picture. Released by 20th Century Fox throughout the United States on 25 May 1979, buoyed up by a massive advertising and merchandising campaign, *Alien* quickly became an 'event' film grossing $60 million dollars in the US alone (by the end of 1998, that figure had grown to an approximate world-wide gross of $164 million). However, Scott's then shocking use of violence, particularly during the seminal 'Chestburster' scene and the sequence where the robotic 'Ash', played by Ian Holm, has his head literally knocked off his shoulders, proved controversial to some. This reaction still irritates the director today.

My main fear during production was always that we'd gone too far with the violence, even though I knew that what I was making was, on one level, a vicious shocker. Still, I never wanted to jar people out of the film because of its viscera. In fact, I'd really wanted to back *off* the hard-core blood and gore for *Alien*. Which is why I was so angry when someone wrote that *Alien* was a manipulative piece of blood and guts movie-making with no redeeming features whatsoever. Excepting the Chestburster sequence, *Alien* is almost totally *devoid* of blood and gore. What these critics missed was the total environment of that film. How artists like H.R. Giger and Ron Cobb had contributed to an environment which had been carefully designed and very carefully thought out. To a large extent, [*Alien*'s] environment was a statement. And, I think, a great piece of art work.

Alien was also to mark the first time Scott was accused of favouring image over content, of creating films marred by thin stories and shallow characters. While *Alien*'s plot is admittedly thin, the execution of that story is not. And the human behaviour on view in *Alien* is actually subtle and naturalistic, hardly the stereotypical histrionics typically encountered in routine genre pictures. As Sigourney Weaver once put it to this writer, *Alien*'s subdued acting style was 'probably misinterpreted by some critics who weren't used to that type of realistic ensemble performance in a science fiction film'. Scott himself continues that line of thought by adding, 'I think a lot of people missed the dynamics of the film during their first screening. *Alien* is always being criticized as being light on characterization, but I think that is totally wrong. The characters were beautifully defined, particularly within the content of the story. Giler and Hill had written just enough of a subtext to each character to let you immediately know who was who, and *Alien*'s cast then very intelligently fleshed those characters out with their own contributions. So, actually, I think I succeeded on that level. In fact, I guess I basically nailed most of what I was after on *Alien*. I mean, it's still a pretty good movie today, right?'

1979 audiences certainly thought so, finding Scott's film involving, hypnotic and absorbing. Two decades of viewers since have also welcomed *Alien*'s many intelligent throwaways, like the little jog Ash (Ian Holm) does to warm himself in the cold belly of his ship, or the sarcastic verbal jousting between the *Nostromo*'s crew, or the oddly tactile moment when Harry Dean Stanton takes off his cap to bathe his face in a soothing stream of water spattering down from a tangle of chains overhead. Every frame of *Alien* suggests a sure, guiding intellect; this is one motion picture which not only indicates an encyclopaedic technical knowledge of film-making, but further suggests that its every detail has been thoroughly considered and thought out (including references to the paintings of Francis Bacon – during Hurt's bloody but still astonishing Chestbursting – and to the woodcuts of Gustave Doré – that staggering, wide-angle special-effects shot of Kane dangling above the derelict's egg chamber). As Scott reveals, even the inclusion of a cat onboard the *Nostromo* had 'been written into the script as a plausible motivation for Ripley to go back into *Nostromo* after she'd set its auto-destruct mechanism at the end, when, in actuality, anybody in their right mind would have gotten off that bloody ship as fast as possible. But Ripley goes back to rescue the only other survivor, which happens to be a cat.'

Alien today is a certifiable mainstream classic, a seminal science fiction film whose imagery and plot devices have been eagerly pilfered by dozens of subsequent genre pictures that 'pay homage' (surely a French phrase for 'commit theft'?) by blatantly copying *Alien*'s intricate production designs, its mature approach to character and story, and its successful melding of horror and science fiction elements. And new audiences continue to embrace three other key elements of the film; its suspenseful ambience, the courageous character portrayed by Sigourney Weaver, and the film's absolutely unearthly title creature. Such is *Alien*'s continuing potency, in fact, that Scott's second film spawned a genuine corporate franchise. Three *Alien* sequels have been mounted by 20th Century Fox since the original's release and, as I write this, rumours concerning the launch of a possible *Alien* 5 continue to escalate.

But for Ridley Scott, *Alien*'s fallout was far more personalized. He now had delivered a certified Hollywood blockbuster, with his first 'Hollywood' film; rightly or wrongly, Scott had also gained a reputation as a master of science fiction. A mantle that was to outline the body of his next, even more ground-breaking work.

5 Heavy Metal Metropolis

Those familiar with my 1996 book *Future Noir: The Making of Blade Runner* know that this writer has already produced a comprehensive examination of Scott's 1982 cult classic. Therefore, it seems the height of redundancy (not to mention masochism) to replay a précis of what has gone before. Those seriously interested in *Blade Runner* will find *Future Noir* still available from both HarperPrism and Orion Publishing; what follows here is a more compact account of the making of Scott's third feature.

Since 1965, the year he had founded RSA, Ridley Scott had moved from triumph to triumph, never suffering a major setback as he capped each success with a larger one. By 1980, he had effortlessly conquered the worlds of design, television, commercial advertising and feature film-making, with every indication showing Scott continuing his upward trek as an archetypal 'self-made man'.

How could Scott predict, then, that the Eighties would instead become a time of personal misfortune, film-making setbacks and artistic self-doubt?

Following *Alien*'s release, Scott was very much a 'hot property'. With the short-sighted logic still prevalent in Hollywood today, the film industry had ignored *The Duellists* and instead opted to peg Scott as a master of frightening, crowd-pleasing, visually brilliant science fiction pictures (the irony that Ridley Scott had no special interest in or commitment to the genre notwithstanding). To be fair, this perception was partly created by the director himself, as Scott (perhaps with tongue in cheek) decided to capitalize on his celebrity by telling various interviewers following *Alien*'s release that he 'wouldn't mind becoming the John Ford of science fiction'.

Thus, when Scott was approached in late 1979 by Italian mega producer Dino De Laurentiis to direct another science fiction film – this one an epic – no one was surprised when he accepted the assignment. De Laurentiis, in the late Seventies, had gained a reputation as a successful presenter of glossy 'A-list' event movies like 1975's *Three Days of the Condor* and 1976's critically reviled but fiscally fruitful *King Kong* remake. The project he was offering Scott was a big-budget version of Frank Herbert's *Dune*, the same ecologically oriented SF novel that Alejandro Jodorowsky had unsuccessfully attempted to adapt. Scott, intrigued by the opportunity 'to literally create entire worlds', found *Dune* both dramatically fascinating and an art director's dream, and, by early 1980, had commissioned a *Dune* script from maverick screenwriter Rudolph Wurlitzer (*Two Lane Blacktop, Pat Garrett and Billy the Kid*).

'But after seven months I dropped out of *Dune*,' Scott continues. 'By then Rudy Wurlitzer had come up with a first-draft script which I felt was a decent distillation of Frank Herbert's (book). But I also realized *Dune* was going to take a lot more work – at least two and a half years' worth. And I didn't have the heart to attack that because my [older] brother Frank unexpectedly died of cancer while I was prepping the De Laurentiis picture. Frankly, that freaked me out. So first I went to Dino and told him the *Dune* script was his. Then I concentrated on RSA for a short while. After that, I got restless. I realized I needed even more activity to get my mind off my brother's death, so I started looking around for another film.'

Even though Scott had not particularly wanted to do another science fiction picture following *Alien* – 'besides a good story, the first thing I look for in a potential project is whether it takes me into a new genre, because I hate repeating myself' - the next screenplay to catch his interest *was* science fiction. This was entitled *Dangerous Days*. Set in a futuristic metropolis, *Days* involved a world-weary detective named Rick Deckard saddled with the unsavoury job of tracking down and executing rogue androids, simulacra who are perfect replicas of human beings but have a vastly shortened lifespan.

The *Days* script was based on a novel (*Do Androids Dream of Electric Sheep?*) by Philip K. Dick, the master of paranoid SF. Its screenplay adaptation had been written by Hampton Fancher, a former MGM contract actor and television performer. 'Besides Hampton's execution of the script, which was remarkable, I was drawn to the moral content of his screenplay,' says Scott. 'Its central conceit was the idea of an officially sanctioned killer murdering what were, after all, really people, even if they were synthetically developed and superior ones. I was also fascinated by this script's graphic possibilities. *Days* crossbred a *noir* film with a police story with a science fiction, and I could sense a lot of opportunities in that hybrid. *Dangerous Days* seemed to present the possibility of doing what I called "layering" back then, the building up of carefully chosen details to create a fully imagined world.'

Ironically, Scott had previously passed on the same screenplay when it was presented to him a year earlier under the title *Android*. Scott's rejection was based on his commitment to *Dune* (ultimately lensed as a fractured, fascinating film by David Lynch, in *1984*), and on his insistence that he didn't want to do another SF film so soon after *Alien*. But Scott's associate Ivor Powell read the *Android* script, was excited by it, and continued to endorse Fancher's screenplay as a possible project. When the retitled *Android* was again presented to Scott by Michael Deeley, a respected English producer (*The Deer Hunter, Convoy*) serving the same function on *Dangerous Days*, Scott reread the piece and altered his initial position, declaring *Dangerous Days* 'an extraordinary piece of work with marvellous design possibilities'.

Ridley Scott officially signed on to his next project – which would be retitled once again, this time as *Blade Runner* – on 21 February 1980. Yet from almost its outset, the production was plagued with a near-Jobian barrage of escalating misfortunes.

BR was originally set to be produced as a modest $13 million effort from Filmways, a mid-tier company that had absorbed and arisen from the corpus of the recently disbanded American-International Pictures, haven of drive-in schlock and Roger Corman classics. But by December 1980, Filmways had suffered a series of costly box-office flops, and the company dropped *Blade Runner* from its production schedule only a month before *BR*'s principal photography was set to begin. Original screenwriter Hampton Fancher (who, along with ex-*Flipper* actor Brian Kelly, served as *Blade Runner*'s Executive Producer) then had a creative falling out with Scott. Fancher was replaced by writer David (*Unforgiven*) Peoples. *Electric Sheep* author Dick next went public with an unhappy reaction to the *Sheep* adaptation, acidly stating, 'I read two drafts of Fancher's screenplay, both bearing the Filmways imprint, and it was just one terrible script. Corny, extremely maladroit throughout.'

Scott and company weathered these initial squalls, however, and by the end of 1980 producer Deeley had secured an eventual *BR* budget of approximately $28 million through a complicated three-way deal involving US studio Warner Brothers, Hong Kong cinema mogul Sir Run Run Shaw, and American television/film production company Tandem Productions (owned by writer/director Bud Yorkin, director Norman Lear and producer Jerry Perenchio). *Blade Runner*'s principal photography period was then reslated to begin 9 March 1981, to last for approximately 16 weeks, and mostly take place on the Burbank-based Warners Studio backlot, which Scott intended to totally transform into a teeming recreation of a densely populated Los Angeles circa 2019. This imaginary city would be overlaid with the drizzle of a constant acid rain, impossibly congested streets, and the looming presence of the same type of brooding, dizzyingly Gothic skyscrapers created for Fritz Lang's *Metropolis* (a key influence on the final look of *Blade Runner*, as Scott told this writer in 1981). Scott also intended to add a sociological shading to *Blade Runner* by showing that 2019 Los Angeles was mostly populated by Asians – a concept which would have seemed perfectly logical in 1981 (given Japan's then rising position in the global economy and the influx of other Asian basin nationalities), but has subsequently been shouldered aside by California's pre-eminence as the number-one population centre for Latinos in the United States.

As he had previously done with Georges de La Tour for *The Duellists* and H.R. Giger/Ron Cobb for *Alien*, Scott now began researching contemporary and classical artists to serve as inspirations for his exotic yet totally convincing 21st century LA. First he (again) turned to *Heavy Metal*, for general visual stimulation. Next the director picked such disparate painters as the Dutch classicist Vermeer and the mid-20th-century artist Edward Hopper on which to model certain *Blade Runner* sequences. More important to the overall look of the production was Scott's discovery of an art book named *Sentinel*, which collected the polished, almost photographically precise 'future technology musings' of artist Syd Mead.

Mead had started his career as a commercial artist working for the Ford Motor Company and Philips Electronics; his speciality lay in designing automobiles and other vehicles that spanned the entire spectrum of the transportation field (Mead helped design the supersonic Concorde airliner, for example). 'Not only could I come up with advanced designs that weren't impossible,' Mead is quoted as saying in *Future Noir: The Making of Blade Runner*, 'but I could also project them into a complete, imaginary scenario... In other words, I was producing little self-contained worlds, automobiles that were placed into fully functioning futuristic environments.'

Mead's talents formed a perfect marriage with the abilities and tastes of Ridley Scott. After being originally hired to provide the design of *Blade Runner*'s flying police car (dubbed a 'Spinner'), Mead had his responsibilities expanded, and he soon found himself creating sets, machinery and other futuristic vehicles for the film. Nevertheless, even though Lawrence G. Paull was also hired as *Blade Runner*'s Production Designer, producer Michael Deeley notes, 'It was really Ridley who generated and created or filtered the overall look of the picture. We did have many different art directors on the project, guys who would just design a cart or something, to be put in the background. But even Syd Mead's work had to pass through Ridley's creative radar. I know film is a collaborative medium, and I certainly don't say this to take anything away from the hard work everyone else gave to the picture. But it was really Ridley Scott who designed *Blade Runner*.'

In addition to Mead, Paull and Deeley, *Blade Runner* also employed a crew whose numbers included celebrated technicians like Jordan Cronenweth (Director of Photography) and editor Terry Rawlings (fresh from *Alien*), while John Chambers (*Planet of the Apes*) and Michael Westmore (*Star Trek: Voyager*) both provided uncredited special make-up effects. Scott then hand-picked Greek-born electronic composer Vangelis (*Chariots of Fire*) to compose *Blade Runner*'s score. As the director says, 'Music has always been an exceptionally important element of film-making to me. Music is a very visual medium, oddly enough. I find I get many mental pictures from music, and therefore, if you put the right music with the right picture, you have lift-off. I also think music can clearly sometimes supplement what you may not have got. Or take you into the fourth dimension with what you have. Which is

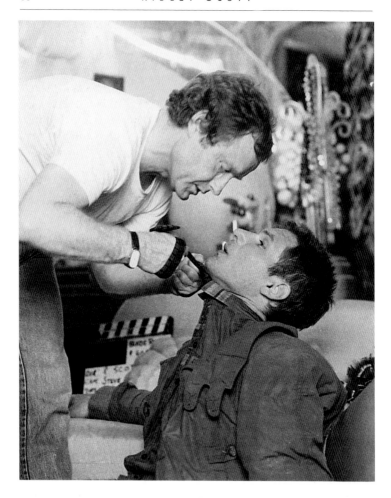

Scott originally wanted Dustin Hoffman for the role of Deckard, but eventually decided on Harrison Ford. However, the relationship between the star and director disintegrated: Ford felt that the director cared more for the sets than for the actors' performances.

exactly what Vangelis did with his score on *Blade Runner*.'

As for casting, Scott had originally wanted Dustin Hoffman for the pivotal role of Deckard. But after a short period of consideration Hoffman was supplanted by Harrison Ford, whom Scott had admired since noticing the actor's small part as a menacing executive assistant in Coppola's *The Conversation* (of course, Ford had also recently become eminently bankable through his star turns in *Raiders of the Lost Ark* and the first two *Star Wars* pictures). Rachael, a synthetic female 'replicant' with whom Deckard falls in love, was portrayed by one-time model and budding actor Sean Young, whom Scott described as looking 'physically perfect, as if she'd just stepped out of a vat' (Scott picked the term 'replicant' over 'android', by the way, because he felt the latter word carried too many negative connotations of cheap exploitation pictures). Darryl Hannah was also picked to portray another replicant, the murderous 'pleasure unit' Pris. Dutch performer Rutger Hauer then rounded out *Blade Runner*'s cast as Roy Batty, the leader of five replicants who have returned to Earth from an 'off-World colony' in order to find a way to extend their limited four-year lifespans.

Just before the start of principal photography, *Blade Runner* had all the hallmarks of another commercial blockbuster. The Warner Brothers backlot, where much of the film was shot (excluding such genuine Los Angeles locations as the Bradbury Building and Ennis-Brown House), had been impressively transformed into a jaw-dropping representation of a dense, hive-like, neon-encrusted 'futureopolis', and, in the early Eighties, big-budget science fiction films were rapidly becoming the viewing public's genre of choice. The *BR* production company had also acquired the remarkable special-effects services of Douglas Trumbull (*2001*, *The Andromeda Strain* and *Star Trek: The Motion Picture*), while the film's adult, provocative storyline was being ably carried by Ford, who delivered one of his finest performances in *Blade Runner*.

But by the third day of production, the film was two weeks behind schedule. Scott and his DP had clashed over the lighting of the first scene shot for the film (the 'emotional lie-detector' test given by Ford to Young), and this footage was completely scrapped in favour of reshooting the sequence. The personal relationship between Ford and co-star Young then quickly deteriorated, and *Blade Runner*'s star fell out with his director, who Ford felt was spending far too much time fine-tuning the film's staggering sets rather than focusing on the actor's own performance. Others on the *BR* crew also began actively resenting Scott's personality, feeling it to be aggressive, insensitive and manipulative. In reference to the American humourist, Will Rogers, famous for claiming he'd never met a man he didn't like, T-shirts were consequently printed up proclaiming 'Will Rogers Never Met Ridley Scott'.

The focus of this controversy was also going through a torturous phase of his own professional life. *Blade Runner* was the first film Scott had shot in Los Angeles under the strict, sometimes Byzantine mandates of the American film unions; one such dictum forbade him to act as his own camera operator. Scott bristled at this restriction, calling such regulations 'illogical, like taking Arnold Palmer's golf clubs away from him'. This is how Scott, with hindsight, sums up the problem:

> I'd walked into a system here that I didn't understand. I think it's probably important to say that. I also walked into a hierarchy that I'd never experienced before, even though I'd done two quite successful movies. But I certainly did-n't go into *Blade Runner* looking to be difficult. In fact, I went in with a cam-eraman whom I'd looked long and hard for, Jordan Cronenweth, who'd been the DP on a film that I quite liked the look of called *Cutter and Bone* [aka *Cutter's Way*]. Jordan, I think it's fair to say, was one of the great American cameramen of the last twenty, twenty-five years. And of course he carried an appropriate team. So when I tried to operate on *BR* I was kind of redundant. Still, that's what I was used to doing. But the American Cinematographer's Guild and some of Jordan's crew were very hard about that, although they gradually softened their stance. Now I usually line up the shots and operate A or B camera on my films, Hollywood picture or not.

Scott's primary nemesis on the film, however, became Tandem Productions. This firm had originally come in as a completion bond guarantor on the picture, and once *Blade Runner* inched over bud-get (towards the end of principal photography), Tandem took the project away from Scott and Deeley and placed Bud Yorkin in nom-inal control of *BR* instead. But Yorkin had vastly different sensi-bilities from Scott's, resulting in constant battles over the film's content, its off-again, on-again voice-over narration, and its origi-nal downbeat ending, which initially left the fate of Deckard and

When Blade Runner **ran over budget, Scott was forced by the production company to add voice-over narration and a happy ending. The final shot, of Harrison Ford and Sean Young escaping into a lush mountain landscape, was composed from out-takes from** The Shining**.**

Rachael uncertain. After a series of disastrous sneak previews, however, Tandem asked for – and Scott provided – a compromised happy ending, showing Ford and Young escaping into a beautiful mountain landscape (actually out-takes from *The Shining*).

Furthermore, the lack of reliance on Scott's creative/technical abilities which, like a toxic undercurrent, had tainted the experience of making *Alien*, now resurfaced tenfold on *Blade Runner*. The result was that Scott frequently became a short-tempered and very loud presence on the *Blade Runner* set.

By the time I made *Blade Runner* I was in overdrive [the director says]. My
company [RSA] was going great on the side, and I've always thought that that
should have at least suggested that I knew how to run a business. And how
to be fiscally responsible. *Alien* seemed to have pretty conclusively found its
audience, too, which you would think would indicate that I know how to craft
an entertainment. But by the time I got into my third film, *Blade Runner*, I was
again questioned so often about everything I did or wanted to do that the situation really pissed me off. That's when I became a screamer. I simply got fed
up answering stupid questions. Things like, 'Why do you want the walls of
Taffy Lewis's nightclub [a decadent 'downtown' *BR* establishment which
Deckard visits during his replicant hunt] painted gold? Why the hell have you
got a unicorn [which appears during a dream sequence and suggests Deckard
is a replicant himself] in this motion picture?' The doubting and interference
and questioning never stopped on *Blade Runner*. Finally, I refused to take it
any more. I'd snap, 'This is the way I want it – just do it!'

Matters became so strained between Tandem, Scott and Deeley, in
fact, that during the film's editing phase, Scott and Deeley were
fired from the production. The pair were quickly reinstated, though,
and despite the resentment Scott aroused in some of his cast and
crew members, there were still those eager to jump to his defence.
'Ridley [can be] a hard taskmaster when he's shooting, I suppose,'
says *BR* editor Terry Rawlings. 'He's very tenacious about what he
wants. Yet I've always gotten along well with him. I like him. I also
have a tremendous regard for talent when I see it. Ridley has that
talent. Plenty of it. Which goes a long way towards soothing whatever temporarily ruffled feelings I might have during a shoot.'

Still, as Scott admits today with a shake of the head, 'I took some
serious body blows on *Blade Runner*. In fact, towards the end, I
was on the ropes spittin' in the bucket.'

Scott's feelings of isolation became even more acute when, after
its May release, *Blade Runner* became one of the first certifiable
flops of the 1982 summer, initially earning only a paltry $14.5 mil-
lion. Audiences expecting another Harrison Ford action-fest were
totally non-plussed to encounter their favourite new actor as a dour
killer in a slowly paced dystopia, who shot women in the back.
Scott's defence today for picking such a downbeat, melancholy
story? 'I tend to like dark subjects,' the director replies with a
shrug.

The *Blade Runner* story does, however, have a happy ending. Its rediscovery on cable TV, videocassette and in revival houses revealed not only a cult film par excellence, but an emotionally challenging, thematically complex work whose ideas and subtexts are just as startling as its justly famous production designs. For if *Alien* rocked people's preconceptions of what a science fiction film could 'look' and 'play' like, *Blade Runner* knocked those preconceptions on their arse. Scott's third motion picture is a haunting, hypnotic, harrowing achievement, one whose overwhelming visuals are strongly linked to its ideas – provocative, multi-textured ones, each subversively embedded in the understructure of what appears to be a mainstream Hollywood product. *BR* may be narratively flawed and (at times) precariously self-indulgent, but it is also remains one of the truly lustrous jewels in Scott's creative crown, a cinematic milestone whose basic integrity, force of imagination and ideological sophistication forever altered the face of contemporary science fiction cinema.

Today, however, Scott prefers to discuss real-world changes wrought by the film. 'One of the major visual ideas we had for *BR* was "retrofitting", this overlaying of pre-existing architecture with patch jobs that sidestep the problem of tearing down old structures and replacing them with new ones. Oddly enough, what I think *Blade Runner* really did – and I can only talk about it now because I did the film so long ago – but today I see a curve in serious architecture which I think started with *Blade Runner*. So we didn't just influence films, we influenced certain types of architecture. And that influence has become very sophisticated. *Blade Runner* spawned a very specific type of industrial beauty.'

Still, in late 1982, Ridley Scott was smarting from the most gruelling film-making experience of his career. In a sense, that same career had been turned upside down, for the huge box-office receipts and popular adulation greeting *Alien* seemed dim phantasms compared with *Blade Runner*'s high-profile lack of financial success. Such a radical reversal of Scott's fortunes could surely explain why, by the end of 1982, the director had secretly begun to question some of the very qualities which had helped him attain his past triumphs.

6 Fairies with Clipped Wings

Ridley Scott's confidence and career appeared unaffected by the *Blade Runner* travails. His services remained in high demand, and two projects which Scott helmed immediately following *BR* presently command cult followings in their own right.

One began production in 1983. That was the year RSA was approached by Chiat/Day, an influential American advertising agency, to shoot a television commercial for an addition to the Apple Computer line, called Macintosh. This new product's primary appeal lay in its revolutionary user interface: one operated a 'Mac' by simply mouse-clicking graphics on its monitor screen, rather than by typing in the tedious codes then required to run Microsoft DOS-based computers. And since Chiat/Day's Macintosh advertisement was intended as the opening salvo of a major marketing campaign, the first Mac commercial – which Scott was signed to direct – was scheduled for broadcast during the January 1984 Superbowl game. Such positioning ensured maximum audience exposure, since this annual American football event still commands exceptionally high TV ratings.

As for concept, Scott's Macintosh commercial was conceived both as a take-off on George Orwell's dystopian novel *1984* and as a dig at IBM, then the largest of Apple's rivals for the home PC market. The ad begins with a single file of shaven-headed workers robotically marching through a futuristic transit tube into a large auditorium. Here rows of other identically dressed workers sit staring listlessly at an enormous television screen. On it looms the bespectacled face of 'Big Brother' (or, by inference, IBM), ranting to his captive audience about 'the first glorious anniversary of the

Information Purification Directives'.

A beautiful blond female athlete suddenly races into the auditorium. She is carrying an Olympic hammer, and is being pursued by four visored policemen. Before she can be captured the woman stops, screams and hurls her hammer at the giant TV screen. This explodes in a shower of sparks. A voice-over and text graphic then announces that 'On January 24th, Apple Computer will introduce Macintosh. And you'll see why 1984 won't be like *1984*.'

Scott's Macintosh spot (now commonly referred to as 'the *1984* commercial') was shot in England at Shepperton Studios, on the same 45,000 foot square soundstage (Stage H) where Scott had earlier filmed *Alien*'s exterior planetoid landscapes. As for 'Big Brother's' speech, this was separately videotaped, then superimposed (during post-production) on a large bluescreen that served as the auditorium's 'viewscreen' by the English special effects company Peerless Optical. The dozens of shuffling, bald-headed workers presented a special problem. 'Employing that large a group of proper actors and then shaving their heads would have been prohibitively expensive,' Scott explains. 'So to keep costs down, we hired 200 non-actors – skinheads – from a group you'd basically call "National Front". They already had shaved heads.'

Scott's mention of cost concerns belies the relative lavishness of the first-ever Macintosh commercial, whose visual panache has led many to assume that its budget was commensurately extravagant. The 1999 edition of *The Guinness Book of World Records*, in fact, claims Scott's Mac commercial is 'The World's Most Expensive TV Ad', and goes on to say: '[Ridley Scott's] commercial for computer manufacturer Apple Macintosh cost $600,000 to produce and $1 million to air.' Yet while Apple did indeed pay $1 million to *air* their advertisement during the Superbowl, the actual *budget* for Scott's '*1984*' commercial was, according to the director, 'nowhere near what's claimed. Actually, that whole Mac spot was done for $350,000. But I guess some people didn't know that. Because there used to be this slightly irritating thing going around that said, "If you've got a million dollars for a commercial, you can take it to Ridley Scott." Well, of course any commercial will look good for a million dollars. But my Mac ad was really done for about a third of that.'

Whatever its budget, Scott's '*1984*' commercial obviously left its

mark on America's consciousness. For despite the fact that it was
televised once (and only once), Scott's Mac ad today is a popular
Internet 'download', and it also appears as a secret 'hack' in commercial software like the Macintosh version of the *Duke Nukem 3-
D (Atomic Edition)* computer game. Here, if one types in a secret
code (DN*1984*) while inside the movie theatre found on *Duke
Nukem*'s first level (the 'Hollywood Holocaust'), a girly film will
transform itself into Scott's Macintosh spot. Such *homages* lend
credence to the opinion set forth in the 1999 *Guinness Book*, which
goes on to state that 'the... impact [of Scott's Mac ad] was so great
and [its] recall among viewers so high that it is believed to be one
of the most cost-effective commercials ever made.'

The final cult favourite Ridley Scott directed during the 1980s
was his fourth motion picture. This, of course, followed *Alien* and
Blade Runner, both of which had cemented the public's perception
of Scott as a visionary science fiction film-maker. Yet Scott himself
insists:

> I wasn't all that interested in science fiction. I'd also been very disappointed
> with the initial impact of *Blade Runner*. Here I thought I'd done a rather unique
> picture, but it wasn't received well, and while I was making it, I'd sometimes
> felt completely on my own.
>
> But I am attracted to exotic subjects [Scott continues]. And in 1982, I still
> wanted to do a medieval fantasy, one that would have the same kind of 'no
> time, no place' feel I'd originally planned for *Tristan and Isolde*. The type of
> fantasy that would lie somewhere between Cocteau's *Beauty and the Beast*
> (1946) – which I love and is truly esoteric – and the Hollywood version of *A
> Midsummer Night's Dream* (1935), with James Cagney and Mickey Rooney. I
> also wanted to make something a little lighter, since my first three films were
> rather intense and heavy. So I attempted something a bit more traditional for
> my fourth film. Something children and everybody else could go see.

The beginnings of Scott's *Blade Runner* follow-up also arose from
the director's desire to generate the subject-matter of his next project himself.

> I was once accused of never developing my own films. What people don't
> understand about me is that I've actually developed over 60 per cent of the
> material that I have made. Which I think is quite a high ratio. Many other

directors just fly with the ball and take what's around.

Anyway, I began looking for material for my fourth film in 1982, right after *Blade Runner*. Around that time I'd read a slender book called *Symbiography* (1973), that had been written by a novelist and poet named William Hjortsberg [also author of the grim 1971 science fiction novel *Grey Matters* and the 1978 occult thriller *Falling Angel*, filmed in 1987 by Alan Parker as *Angel Heart*]. Since I liked *Symbiography* very much, I got hold of Hjortsberg on the telephone. That went well so I met Gatz, as people call him, in New York, where I told him what I wanted my next movie to be about. And then, during a later telephone conversation, the basic idea for something we originally called *Legend of Darkness* came about.

Thirteen years after its 1986 American release, *Legend of Darkness* (later shortened to *Legend*) is generally perceived as Ridley Scott's most severely compromised work. It is also the most difficult to criticize objectively, since, in its current form(s), *Legend* is so choppily edited that its director's true intentions are almost impossible to assess. Paradoxically, *Legend* is also the latest Scott project to begin, *à la Blade Runner*, to show signs of heightened audience interest after an initially disappointing release. In fact, demand is mounting for a *Legend* 'Director's Cut', and several retrospective articles about the film have recently appeared in various cinema magazines. Yet Scott himself has remained relatively quiet on the subject of *Legend*. At least until now – which explains the following, fairly lengthy coverage of what is, at least in its present form, a frustratingly disjointed work.

Once Scott and Hjortsberg had worked out a rough outline for *Legend*, the writer joined Scott in Los Angeles, where the director ran Cocteau's *Beauty and the Beast* for Hjortsberg one Saturday morning at a screening room inside the Beverly Hills Hotel. 'The Cocteau basically knocked Gatz's socks off,' Scott continues. 'But *Beauty and the Beast* was only *part* of what I wanted us to do. So I told Gatz, "We've really got to reinvent this whole area. Not so much the fantasy genre, but what's inside of it. Let's aim for something relatively complex, even if it is a fairy-tale."'

The fairy-tale Hjortsberg and Scott had conceived for *Legend* mixed elements of classical European folk tales (such as those collected by the Brothers Grimm) with Judeo-Christian myth. Its action primarily took place within a beautiful forest, a mystical 'enchanted wood' harbouring a beautiful young princess called Lili, a 'forest boy' named Jack, plus assorted animals, elves, fairies and goblins. Also in attendance are the world's last two unicorns, which a malevolent horned demon named 'Darkness' plots to kill, for the death of these divine creatures will cause perpetual night to fall upon the Earth. Lili and Jack, of course, become heroic foils to the evil Darkness's plan. But after Lili is kidnapped and corrupted by the cunning demon, Jack must not only ensure the unicorns' safety, but rescue his Princess as well.

William Hjortsberg would spend over two years (from 1982 to 1984) writing 15 drafts of his *Legend* screenplay. During this period, Scott's wish for a *dark* fairy-tale would result in such discarded ideas as Lili and Darkness having sex, or an unfilmed scene showing the Princess transforming into a half-woman, half-cat creature after her fall from grace. Scott desired such moments 'because despite how she comes across now in *Legend*, which is innocence personified, Lili was nevertheless conceived as being very manipulative. Basically, she was a brat. A lot of that was edited out of the final film, though. Which bothered me later on, because I'd always felt it was Lili's manipulative streak that let her be seduced to the side of evil. The film as released doesn't give you much sense of that.'

Lili's seduction was eventually visualized by showing the Princess dancing with a bewitched gown; this empty garment (animated by Darkness) chills the young woman's heart, after it has magically moulded itself around her body. But such sequences could only have been properly staged with sufficient funding, which had only been secured for *Legend* after a two-way deal was struck (in 1984) between Universal Pictures and 20th Century Fox. Under the terms of this agreement, Universal retained *Legend*'s North American distribution rights, while Fox became the film's overseas rights holder. The film's budget was then set at $25 million, and Arnon Milchan signed on as *Legend*'s Producer.

Alex Thomson, a superb British cinematographer whose work for the 1980 Arthurian epic *Excalibur* was much admired by Scott, was picked to be *Legend*'s Director of Photography. Also dotting the *Legend* crew were a number of former Scott collaborators. Among them were Terry Rawlings, *Legend*'s Editor, as well as Jerry Goldsmith (the film's composer), Special Effects Supervisor Nick

Allder, Dubbing Editor Jim Shields (who'd previously created eerie sound effects for *Alien* and *Blade Runner*), and Costume Designer Charles Knode (co-creator of *BR*'s wardrobe). However, long-time associate Ivor Powell, who had line-produced Scott's first three films, was not involved with *Legend*. Powell had moved from feature film-making after *Blade Runner* to concentrate on television commercials instead.

As usual, Ridley Scott depended heavily on storyboards and real-world artists to stimulate the designs of his latest venture. For example, over 400 pages of *Legend* storyboards were generated for the film, drawing on a variety of sources, as Scott recalls:

I looked very carefully at the work of Arthur Rackham prior to shooting *Legend* [Rackham, a late 19th/early 20th century British artist, was famed for his fairy-tale and children's book illustrations]. We also brought in a guy named Alan Lee to provide some conceptual art for the film. Lee had earlier worked with the artist Brian Froud, on a book called *Fairies*. But the way I wanted Darkness to look was locked in before Lee arrived. Darkness's physical appearance was based on the winged-and-horned demon from *Fantasia* [the 1940 Disney film], which you see during the 'Night on Bald Mountain' segment. I'd always felt that that part of *Fantasia* was pretty bloody scary, you know? So our Darkness was sort of a nod towards that. Although I suppose it's really more honest to say that my Darkness was modelled after William Blake. Because Blake's art certainly was an influence on Disney's 'Night on Bald Mountain'!

To actualize *Legend*'s 'enchanted wood', Scott first explored locations in northern California's famed Redwood forest, with an eye towards making it his primary filming site. Later, however, the director chose to *build* an artificial forest. This enormous construct was housed within what was then the world's largest soundstage, the '007 stage' at England's Pinewood Studios, so-called because it was built for the 1977 James Bond film *The Spy Who Loved Me*. In fact, dozens of live trees, a running brook, a bear, numerous shrubs, horses, bees, flowers, small animals and a ten-foot deep pond were spread out inside the 007 stage before Scott was satisfied that *Legend* Production Designer Assheton Gorton (who took 16 weeks to complete the task) had created the ultimate magic forest.

'Actually, the general design of *Legend*'s woods was based on a huge forest set that had been built [in Germany] for *Siegfried*, the [1924] Fritz Lang film,' Scott adds, 'for a scene where Siegfried kills a dragon.'

Obviously, the early 'architectural cinema' of Fritz Lang has been a key influence on the films of Ridley Scott, since, in addition to *Legend*, Langian elements also appear in Scott's '*1984*' commercial and *Blade Runner* (whose omnipresent 'shafts of light', incidentally, were not derived from Lang, but from lighting effects Scott had noticed during the 'Newsreel Screening Room' and 'Thatcher Library' sequences of *Citizen Kane*). One *Legend* technique created solely by Ridley Scott, however, involved the ubiquitous 'floating fluff' seen wafting through *Legend*'s woodlands.

According to the director, this material was really 'minced-up duck down. I decided to have that stuff everywhere because, when you are in a real forest during the spring, there are usually things floating through the air all the time. So one day I had somebody bring me a pillow with duck feathers in it. We chopped that up, then blew it through the Bond stage. Against the backlight, it looked like we had millions of seeds floating through the forest. We used about a hundredweight of feathers for that.'

Legend's performers were, like the cast of *Alien* before them, a mixture of American and European thespians. The then relatively unknown Tom Cruise, whom Scott had seen in *Taps* (1981) and *Risky Business* (1983), was cast as the heroic Jack o' the Green. The director then arranged a screening of Truffaut's 1970 film *The Wild Child* for the young actor, 'to give Tom an idea of the feral quality I had in mind for Jack'. For Princess Lili, Scott picked Mia Sara, an aspiring English performer 'we hired straight out of drama school'. Gump, the courageous elf who helps Lili and Jack during their quest, was portrayed by German actor David Bennent, who had previously earned critical kudos for his central performance in Volker Schlondorff's 1979 *The Tin Drum*. Blix, the androgenous Goblin who becomes Lili and Jack's running foil, was played by Alice Playten, who also dubbed David Bennent's lines owing to post-production fears that Bennent's German accent was too thick for American audiences. Rounding out *Legend*'s supporting cast were longtime American character actor/ 'little person' Billy Barty (as the comical Screwball), English performer Annabelle Layton (playing the exotic, Tinkerbell-like Oona), and American Robert

Picardo (now best known as *Star Trek: Voyager*'s holographic 'Doctor'); Picardo essayed the grotesque, man-eating 'Swamp Hag' Meg Mucklebones.

'Casting the role of Darkness was particularly tricky,' Scott recalls. 'It was an oversize role hanging on a fine line that could have easily tipped over into pretentiousness. That got me thinking about performers who could get away with Darkness's unique blend of menace and humour. Then I remembered Tim Curry, who played [Dr Frank N. Furter] in *The Rocky Horror Picture Show*.' Curry easily walks away with the bulk of *Legend*'s acting honours, since his Darkness is simultaneously sardonic, unpredictable, sensual and intense. Darkness is also one of the most majestic villains in Scott's *oeuvre*, an antagonist every bit the equal of the tortured-yet-childlike Roy Batty, played by Rutger Hauer in *Blade Runner*.

This superb performance was enhanced by remarkable prosthetics courtesy of *Legend*'s Special Make-up Supervisor, Rob Bottin, who in 1984 was principally known for his 'transformation F/X' for *The Howling* (1980) and *The Thing* (1982). Bottin transformed Tim Curry into the quintessential horned demon by first outfitting the actor with fluorescent contact lenses, two satyr-like furred and hoofed feet (which encased 18-inch-long, stilt-like leg extensions, to increase Curry's height), plus lightweight polystyrene horns measuring over three feet in length. The final touch was a dark scarlet make-up Bottin applied over Curry's body.

'Working with Rob was fun,' Scott says today. 'He has a touch of genius. And of course he's a guy who doesn't leave the studio. Rob's always behind you, breathing in your left ear, saying, "I think the gauze is lifting"' [laughs].

Legend began filming on 23 March 1984. Principal photography lasted 21 weeks. Shooting was primarily relegated to Pinewood Studios, although Scott and a small crew did journey to Silver Springs (in Ocala, Florida) to film an underwater sequence of Jack retrieving Lili's ring from the bottom of a pond.

'Funnily enough,' continues Scott, 'making *Legend* was actually rather scary. My confidence was a little uneven, because the scale of everything was so huge.'

A more serious problem arose on 27 June 1984, when the entire 007 stage burned to the ground during a freak fire, taking *Legend*'s extraordinary forest set along with it. 'That happened during lunch-time,' says Scott.

I was in the editing room when somebody came racing in yelling, 'The stage is on fire!' Then I heard helicopters overhead. So I went outside and there were ITN, CNN and BBC helicopters circling over the bloody Bond stage, photographing it as it went up. We'd been using some gas bottles in there to make a fire for a fairy dance I'd been shooting. Those gas bottles were exploding when I came out, making the stage walls ripple like a huge aircraft carrier going down. The guy who'd been on duty when the fire broke out apparently had just sat down outside the stage for lunch when it started. He'd heard a loud pop, ran back inside, stared up at the stage's roof, and seen this tidal wave of fire moving across it. What possibly happened was that a residue of gas fumes had been gradually building up near the ceiling of the Bond stage, which is about 56 feet off the floor. And those fumes weren't being extracted well enough. Then some sort of spark or electrical short ignited them.

Luckily, no one was injured. My biggest headache was that after the fire I still had three weeks of Forest filming left to do, and no Forest left to do it. But Assheton Gorton had got ahead in building his other sets, so we were able to make those work overtime. Assheton's being ahead of the game meant we only lost three shooting days.

Legend's bad luck continued into its preview phase, after Scott's original 113-minute cut of the film did not score well with test audiences. This reaction caused the director to severely rethink, reduce and re-edit his film, an action ultimately resulting in two different versions of *Legend*. Universal's domestic version clocked in at 89 minutes, while Fox's overseas release ran approximately 94. 'I made the European cut slightly longer,' Scott explains, 'because I felt European audiences would be more in sync with what I was trying to accomplish.'

However, the trigger for Scott's decision to cut nearly half an hour from his original *Legend* edit had been that earlier American screening. Scott recalls this as 'a bloody disaster'.

The first preview was held at the Director's Guild, in Los Angeles, with about 400 people. Due to the kinds of movies I make, sometimes I think they pull in a lot of dope heads. And I could smell marijuana during that *Legend* preview. Then somebody started to snigger. That same somebody made a sar-

castic comment, and a whole ripple of other comments followed, which made
me furious. Here's this arsehole in the crowd somewhere with a couple of his
buddies, laughing because they're stoned, disrupting a very important event.
That was very destructive because the general feeling after the preview was
that *Legend* was too sentimental. Which surprised the shit out of me; I didn't
think anything could be too sentimental for the United States. Anyway, if I'm
ever in an important screening again where that sort of thing happens, I'll
stop the show myself, put the lights up, and get rid of the guilty parties.
Because foolishness like that during a studio preview is lethal, I can tell you.

However, Scott's revisions did not stop at the shearing of over 20
minutes from *Legend* between the film's first preview and its final
release. The director also completely replaced the lushly romantic
Jerry Goldsmith score accompanying Fox's overseas version of the
film (albeit in an awkwardly re-edited form) with the hurriedly
commissioned 'New Age'-type music (featuring synthesizer and
flute) that is heard on the American cut. This alternate score was
composed by the German electronic group, Tangerine Dream.

Actually, I felt awful about having to replace Jerry Goldsmith's music on the
American version, because Jerry had given me exactly what I'd asked for [Scott
says]. And I still think Jerry's score for *Legend* was bloody good [it is also still
available, on compact disc, from Silva Screen Ltd]. But somehow, during all
the second-guessing that went on while we were re-editing the film, Jerry's
music began to be perceived as being too sweet; frankly, [Universal] got a little paranoid and thought Jerry's stuff too sentimental. I was persuaded to be
insecure about Goldsmith's score as well. So Tangerine Dream was hired to
rescore the film for America. But comparing the Goldsmith and Tangerine
Dream scores is difficult, because we only had three weeks to do the
Tangerine Dream one. And I do think that what the Dream guys did in the time
they had to do it in was pretty good. But was it as sophisticated as Jerry's
music? No. So it's all very, very sad. Goldsmith was upset by the situation, and
we've never spoken since. After what he went through on *Alien* and then
Legend, I doubt Jerry would want to work with me again.

Despite Scott's mentioning of Universal's 'paranoia', however, the
director is quick to defend that studio's then head of production,
Sid Sheinberg, who at roughly the same time was locked in a bitter
public battle over the re-editing of Terry Gilliam's 1985 film *Brazil*.

Oddly enough, the one person who was the most supportive to me throughout *Legend* was Sid Sheinberg [Scott states emphatically]. We'd sit and watch the film and he'd keep saying, 'There's a goddamn good movie here.' I think the real problem was that the more you preview – which we did on *Legend* – the more dangerous it gets. Because you then start to whittle away at stuff you shouldn't whittle away at. Anyway, I cut a lot of interesting stuff out of *Legend* that I'm now sorry is gone. Basically, I got afraid of the film's rather ingenuous fairy-story emotion. So Sheinberg shouldn't be blamed. The person who ultimately convinced me to cut and rescore *Legend* was myself.

Don't forget, I also was very insecure after *Blade Runner*, where I felt sure I really had something, then watched it fail. That put me into the position of starting to believe what I didn't believe. So another way of explaining what happened on *Legend* was that I was being Hollywood-ized by the reaction to *Blade Runner*. Believe me, I'd have been far more esoteric and highbrow with *Legend* had *Blade Runner* been financially successful. Since it wasn't, I began pulling punches. What happened to me on *Legend* was definitely the result of my own crisis of confidence.

Scott's forebodings were confirmed once the film opened. *Legend* was originally scheduled for American release in June 1985. But the rescoring and re-editing process pushed that date back to 8 November 1985, then May 1986, which is when *Legend* finally made its US premiere – a resoundingly disappointing one. Most audiences found *Legend*'s continuity confusing, critics dismissed the film's storyline (and characters) as 'weak', and Ridley Scott's fourth feature limped out of most American theatres barely one or two weeks after it arrived.

'The film didn't do that great in Europe, either,' says Scott. 'So all the re-editing and score changes were really for nothing.'

Still, despite its limp reception, Scott does feel that *Legend* had its merits. 'I've heard that the film has become very popular on video. That's a testimonial to all involved, really, because the crafts supporting *Legend* really were masterful. In fact *Legend* is, in my opinion, a masterful piece of scenic design. But you know what? Assheton Gorton and the rest of the *Legend* guys didn't get one single Academy Award for what they did. That was absolutely criminal. The films that did get Academy Awards that year for camera or costume or art direction were nowhere in comparison.'

Today *Legend* does indeed seem headed towards some kind of

popular revival, one spearheaded by the same (swelling) home video audience mentioned by Scott. The film also continues to generate more and more Internet websites (including the invaluable '*Legend* FAQ', whose on-line address is http://www.slip.net/~figment/), and Scott himself is toying with the idea of restoring previously deleted footage and Goldsmith's full score to a special *Legend* 'Director's Cut'.

However, despite its current popularity, Scott came off *Legend* in 1986 'basically reeling. I felt like a bruised pineapple. I didn't know what I thought about that film at the end. I kept telling myself that all you can do is cling to getting everything technically as powerful or as delicate as you can make it. So I just made sure that *Legend* looked great, and that the music and everything else was well mixed. After that, I kind of lost it.'

Those familiar with the inner workings of Hollywood might suspect that the consecutive fiscal failures of *Blade Runner* and *Legend* also had seriously threatened Scott's status as an 'A-list' film-maker. Yet while these discouragements did undermine his self-confidence, Scott soon discovered that *Legend*, like *Blade Runner* before it, had not weakened the solid level of respect he still commanded within the motion picture industry. Neither had *Legend*'s failure harmed Scott's position as a major director, able to raise studio financing for his next film, whatever that next film might be.

'What interests me tends to be on a project-to-project basis,' Scott explains. 'Particularly if it falls into whatever genre I haven't tackled yet. So when people ask, "Have you a plan?", I usually say no. 'Then again, if a young director asks what I aim at, I'll tell him, "Forget the box office. Just try to make a great movie. All you can do is try and create a good piece of work."'

7 Urban Temptation, Asian Redemption

One obstruction to a clear-eyed appraisal of the career of Ridley Scott is the assumption that there are only three major films worth discussing in that career – *Alien*, *Blade Runner* and *Thelma and Louise* (although an increasing number of next-generation film buffs might extend that list to include *Legend*). This popular perception has definitely not been challenged by the critical community which, by the late Eighties, was already bemoaning Scott's turning away from the staggeringly detailed science fiction worlds he'd created early in his career towards the more reality-based ones of his later projects.

While such opinions may be understandable on one level – after all, the influence of his second and third films upon popular culture has been enormous – the backlash against Ridley Scott's latest motion pictures seems to have more to do with aesthetic challenge (i.e. Scott now only does large-scale straight work) or a disappointment fuelled by unfulfilled expectations (why doesn't Scott give us more *Aliens* and *Blade Runners* ?), than a willingness to weigh the true quality of that work. The notion that Scott can be considered as a three-hit wonder also appears tainted by certain reactionary undercurrents eddying through popular film criticism. These conservative tendencies often praise artists for returning to the same 'artistic' turf, instead of encouraging them to strike off in new directions.

But such opinions overlook the very real, very human fact that it's always difficult for directors, no matter how talented, to consistently surpass themselves after hitting the jackpot with their first attempts (just ask Orson Welles). Besides, those willing to rewatch *all* of Scott's works (through the authentic technological magic of the 20th century's most invaluable cinematic research tool, the home VCR), may be surprised to discover that there actually are *other* Ridley Scott motion pictures as well executed and satisfying as Scott's better-known 'Big Three'. The overlooked *Duellists*, for example, or *Someone to Watch Over Me*, *Black Rain* and *White Squall*; all seem ripe for rediscovery, and these last two surely would have received far more positive welcomes during their original runs had they not come from the same man who'd previously directed two popular and influential science fiction classics. Furthermore, even Scott's recent projects, flawed or otherwise – *G.I. Jane*, *1492: Conquest of Paradise* – contain passages of sustained brilliance, perfectly realized first, second or third acts whose excellence is unfortunately diluted by the structuring or erratic pacing of the rest of the film.

So perhaps it is (well past?) time to briefly give Ridley Scott's later 'orphan projects' their proper due.

The first of these under-appreciated items is *Someone to Watch Over Me*, an effort which must rank among Scott's warmest, most audience-friendly films. Paradoxically, this motion picture was generated during the film-maker's most restricted creative hour, for if the disappointments and frustrations associated with *Blade Runner* and *Legend* had not damaged Scott's career, they had caused him to adopt a warier approach to his fifth feature film.

'Compared to what I'd already done,' Scott begins, '*Someone to Watch Over Me* was very "normal". I figured I'd better go down a route of being normal after what had happened with *Legend* and *Blade Runner*. Now I've discovered, after hindsight, that I *shouldn't* try to be conventional. Because not many people can do great oddball stuff. I may as well spend 19 months doing a film I really want to do as opposed to 13 months doing a film which I'm doing a good servicing job on. Which, fuck, I can do with my eyes closed.'

Not that *Someone to Watch Over Me* was a cynical service job. By the mid Eighties Scott's successful advertising and business interests had left him financially secure; therefore, he almost always has had the luxury of making only those films 'I feel passionate about', and *Someone to Watch Over Me* was definitely one of those undertakings. The film's basic storyline had been pitched to the director during a 1985 dinner party that included screenwriter

Howard Franklin. According to Scott, 'After Howard told me what he had in mind, I said, "God, I really like that." So we developed *Someone to Watch Over Me* from scratch.'

Lifting its title from George and Ira Gershwin's time-honoured torch song (sung over the film's opening credits by the intelligent rock musician Sting, who, like Scott, hails from the hard climes of northeastern England), *Someone to Watch Over Me* is a romantic thriller complicated by a difficult ethical dilemma. Sophisticated New York socialite Claire Gregory (the always interesting Mimi Rogers) accidently witnesses a brutal murder. She is then threatened by the crime's paranoid perpetrator, Joey Venza (Andreas Katsulas, a heavy-featured actor with the most menacing brow in Hollywood). Next Claire is assigned police protection in the form of Mike Keegan (Tom Berenger), a lower-middle-class detective from Queens.

Keegan enjoys a solid family life, and is happily married to the tough-talking, rough-edged Ellie (Lorraine Bracco). At first he reacts awkwardly to the glamour of Claire's upper-class life, disliking the shallowness of a high society he must temporarily inhabit as 'a baby-sitter for a material witness to a homicide'. But then Keegan slowly finds himself emotionally tempted by his assignment, since Claire is a strong, attractive, intelligent woman with little affectation. And Claire's own attraction towards her protective policeman soon threatens the very marriage Keegan holds dear.

Scott was pitched this storyline during a period when he'd been trying to develop a film at Columbia called *Johnny Utah* (ultimately retitled *Point Break*, and directed by Kathryn Bigelow in 1991). However, unhappiness with *Utah*'s developmental progress caused Scott to take on *Someone* instead.

'What attracted me to Howard Franklin's idea was the situation of a good marriage having this intrusive element, a very tempting one, unexpectedly enter the equation. The Berenger character isn't looking for an affair, but both he and Mimi Rogers are suddenly thrown together into a high-pressure situation which knocks their internal compasses off. I also liked the contrast and coming together of the two main characters' different social classes. Because everyone says there's no class system in the United States, and that's rubbish.'

Scott picked Tom Berenger for the role of Mike Keegan on the strength of Berenger's impressive and contrasting performances in *The Big Chill* and *Platoon*, as well as the fact that 'I find Tom to be a very sympathetic actor'. Rogers and Katsulas were cast during the usual audition process; Lorraine Bracco (whose first film this would be) was offered the role of Ellie, says Scott, because 'I always have a tendency to look for new faces. Although she'd never done any motion picture work before, Lorraine had had a small part in a New York play with Harvey Kietel, and was a very strong newcomer. I met with her, and she was a real character. What you see in that film is exactly who Lorraine is.'

But exactly how does Scott work with his actors? And how does he respond to the recurring criticism that his motion pictures are sometimes more concerned with production and design than with plot or character?

An opinion was brewing around the time I was shooting *Someone to Watch Over Me* [Scott begins] that I didn't like working with actors, and that I tended to make the scenery in my films more important than the actors or scripts. That reaction may have started with *Blade Runner*, when I said that sometimes the design of a film was just as important as its acting or story. Perhaps I was misunderstood there, because I certainly didn't mean *more* important. For instance, I've always tried to attach a reality to what actors create during filming. That's really what my job as a director is, in terms of performance; the actors do it, and I'm there to monitor it. So, ideally, that end of the process should be a partnership, with me as a guidance system. And I've always felt that everything starts with story. In fact, story and performance were two of the main reasons I chose to do *Someone to Watch Over Me* – it had a smaller, more contained story that foregrounded the performances.

Scott spent 11 weeks during the latter half of 1986 shooting *Someone* in Manhattan, Queens, and Los Angeles, where different areas acted as stand-ins for supposed New York locations. For instance, Mimi Rogers' luxurious Manhattan townhouse was actually a set built on a soundstage at the Sony Pictures Studio lot in Culver City, California. *Someone*'s opening party scene was likewise filmed in downtown Los Angeles' Mayan Theater, while its pivotal homicide was shot at a swimming pool inside the *Queen Mary*, the decommissioned luxury liner and popular Long Beach CA tourist attraction. Today Scott recalls the overall experience of filming *Someone* as 'an absolute walk in the park, because the scale of my three previous movies had been so huge. This was a more intimate drama. I also felt comfortable filming in New York, since I'd already done literally hundreds of commercials there. Although I must say shooting on the *streets* of New York is somewhat trying. New Yorkers aren't impressed by film units. They're more inclined to say, "Get that fucking tripod out the way."'

One notable technical achievement in *Someone to Watch Over Me* is its remarkable opening shot, directed by Scott during post-production (from a helicopter – in one take) while the film-maker was otherwise absorbed by *Someone*'s editing process. This long, gorgeous aerial view of the dusky Manhattan skyline not only echoes *Blade Runner*'s inaugural 'Industrial Hellscape' shot, but celebrates New York's famed Chrysler Building, caressing the building in a slow, sensuous circle before sweeping across the Hudson River and coming to rest on the building in Queens that is the home of Mike and Ellie Keegan. 'I've always loved the Chrysler Building,' Scott says. 'From a designer's point of view, it's real fantasy architecture, and one of the most beautiful buildings of its era. In fact, it's more beautiful than the Empire State Building. A spectacular achievement.'

Those criticisms of narrative inconsistency, shallow characterization and emotional coldness that had dogged some of Scott's earlier works should have been laid to rest by *Someone to Watch Over Me*. This is a film that embodies the very antithesis of those complaints; its story is involving, its viewpoint compassionate, and its protagonists are appealing. Moreover, Scott's fifth feature offers a predicament unusual to mainstream movie-making – a 'good' husband who transgresses on his marriage not because of any moral weakness (such as lust or greed), but because of the genuine protectiveness he feels towards the attractive woman whose life literally rests in his hands. Scott himself felt that 'we nailed a good human story in *Someone*, which is what I'd set out to do. I'd also satisfied my own questions about what would happen if I didn't have the settings and scenery of a major production to hide behind.'

Yet in spite of its affectionate characters and the interesting ethical tension straining at the heart of its mature love story, *Someone to Watch Over Me* was a low – perhaps the low – point in Scott's feature film-making career. The film was released with virtually no publicity build-up in 1987 (the victim of a new administrative regime at Columbia Pictures, which did not support the project). It then almost immediately disappeared from the few theatres into which it had been booked, grossing only $10 million during its American release. The few viewers *Someone* did attract seemed to be, for the most part, fans of Scott's big-budget fantasias, and these probably felt let down by 'their' director's apparent willingness to desert the exotic genres which had previously so dazzled them.

Scott himself responded to the brutal fate of his most underrated film with hard-won equanimity. 'By now I was really getting philosophical. I thought, "There goes another one. I did it right, but it didn't really go. Oh well – time to move on to the next case."'

Scott's next case ironically proved to be more like the polished but anonymous thriller many mistakenly perceived *Someone* to be. This was *Black Rain*, a 1989 Paramount action film.

Black Rain's protagonist is Nick Conklin (Michael Douglas), a tough New York cop who has gone 'on the take' because of alimony, child support payments and other financial pressures. Early in the film he is charged with delivering a violent *yakuza* (Japanese gangster) named Sato (Yusaku Matsuda) back to the authorities in Japan; Conklin is accompanied on this trip by his more ethical partner, Charlie Vincent (Andy Garcia). After they land at Osaka airport, however, Sato escapes, and Nick and Charlie are then forced to pursue the criminal on what, to them, is culturally alien turf. But during his visit to Japan Conklin learns the value of honour from Masahiro Matsumoto (Ken Takakura, iconic lead of many Seventies Japanese *yakuza* films, also the co-star of Sydney Pollock's 1975 *The Yakuza*), a self-effacing Japanese detective who assists Nick and Charlie during their search for Sato; at the same time, Matsumoto learns the importance of self-assertion from Nick.

The film containing these interesting cross-cultural currents was, according to Scott, 'The first time I did a motion picture purely as a hired gun. I was only directing *Black Rain*, not producing it, which I'd been doing on various levels as far back as *Blade Runner*. So in a way it was like a busman's holiday. I had a lot of fun on *Black Rain*.'

Rain had been offered to Scott by Paramount executives Sherry Landing and Stanley Jaffe, who'd been forced to find another director for the film after their original choice, Dutch film-maker Paul Verhoeven, turned down *Black Rain* because he felt he could not do proper justice to its 'clashing cultures' subtext. Shooting began on location in Japan (in Osaka) on 28 October 1988. However, after only about six weeks of filming in Osaka and the Japanese port city of Kobe, highly publicized difficulties between the production's Japanese and American elements forced the company to suspend its Japan-based shooting on 8 December 1988.

'I think the main problem we had on *Black Rain* was with us, the American side of the production, misunderstanding the Japanese order,' explains Scott. 'The way they function and the way they work. Which was a real crippler since, for the most part, except for key people like Jon DeBont, who shot the film, I had an entirely Japanese crew. I also think there was a misunderstanding of how costly it would be in Japan. Which was, *very*.'

Scott and Paramount solved this stalemate by moving *Black Rain* back to America in January 1989. Here sequences were shot in Manhattan and New York's Silvercup Studios; areas around Los Angeles and California doubled for the lost Japanese locations. Among these latter locales was northern California's Napa Valley, where, in an area just south of the town of Calistoga, Scott transformed an American vineyard into a Japanese sake farm, where a climactic motorcycle chase and *yakuza* crimelord meeting were shot. The film's principal photography phase then wrapped in a San Francisco suburb on 14 March 1989; a completed *Rain* was released by Paramount on 22 September of the same year.

Black Rain is not without its strong points. One of them is the way in which Scott shoots present-day Osaka as if that city had already become the neon-washed Japanese equivalent of *Blade Runner*'s Los Angeles; equally impressive is Scott's use of more specific Japanese locations, like the two-story driving range Conklin visits to meet a *yakuza* kingpin, a subtly bizarre edifice shouldered up against a nearby elevated freeway. Additionally, when Douglas visits Ken Takakura's home – only to find the Japanese detective living in a tiny, tiny apartment – the sequence quietly captures a constrictive facet of daily Japanese life of which few *gaijin*, or foreigners, are aware. And *Black Rain* also contains the single most thrilling edit in Scott's entire feature career.

During a climactic fist fight, Conklin has the opportunity to impale Sato on a wooden stake rising up from the muddy ground of a *sake* farm. Conklin smiles wolfishly at his enemy, thrusts him backwards towards the stake – and a sudden jumpcut to the interior of the Osaka police station reveals that not only has Conklin let Sato live, but that the formerly tormented New York cop has completed his spiritual redemption by allowing Matsumoto, his loyal Japanese partner, to be the one who triumphantly presents the cowed and manacled Sato to Matsumoto's superior officers.

This is an immensely satisfying moment in *Black Rain*, on both the story and 'pure film-making' levels. Yet Scott had actually originally filmed Sato being *impaled* on this stake, and killed by Conklin. 'But Sherry Lansing and Stanley Jaffe argued that it made more sense dramatically to show Sato having to face legal retribution at the end. Douglas killing Sato also didn't really jibe very well with the idea that Michael's character becomes a better person during his trip to Japan. So I cut out Sato's death scene and shot additional footage, showing Douglas and Ken delivering Sato to the Osaka police.'

The acting by *Black Rain*'s principal performers is also good. Michael Douglas ably conveys a man wrestling with his conscience, while Andy Garcia's uncharacteristically jovial performance is outstanding. So too is Ken Takakura's humble policeman… although anyone who has enjoyed Takakura's earlier *yakuza* films probably wishes that at least one *Black Rain* scene had allowed Ken to display the same explosive physicality that so thrilled Asian audiences during the 1970s.

An equally interesting bit of *Black Rain* casting surrounds the solemn gravity of Japanese performer Tomisaburo Wakayama, who portrays *Black Rain*'s Sugai, a 'Big Boss' *yakuza* overlord to whom Douglas must humble himself before he can bring Sato down; Wakayama (who died in 1995) is given an interesting speech towards the end in which he explains how he hates America, both for detonating nuclear weapons in his homeland and for dominating Japan's post-war cultural landscape. The actor himself was an expert swordsman and long-time Japanese celebrity who had earlier become a cult favourite for his six-picture stint as Ogami Itto, a former Imperial Executioner forced to wander medieval Japan as a penniless mercenary, while wheeling his infant son in a wooden baby cart.

Michael Douglas with Scott on the set of Black Rain. **Even though portions of the film were shot on location in Los Angeles and California, Scott still manages to recreate the atmosphere of Osaka, presenting it as a Japanese verson of** Blade Runner's **Los Angeles.**

According to Ridley Scott, securing the services of Tomisaburo Wakayama – then regarded, like Ken Takakura, as a living legend in Japan – was not easy. 'My first meeting with Tommy [Wakayama] was very interesting,' Scott says. 'Stars like him are kind of a law unto themselves in Japan, really. He was very formal during our first meeting, which is when I asked him to be in *Black Rain*. Someone was sitting on one side of Tommy lighting a cigarette every ten minutes and setting it into his cigarette holder. So our talk was very impressive, actually. Also a little weird. Like a drama being acted out, even though it was a normal meeting, as far as I could gather. Anyway, Tommy just nodded at everything I said. Finally, at the end, he muttered something to the translator in Japanese, which meant, "Yes, I'll do it." And that was it.'

Overshadowing these other *Black Rain* performers, however, is Yusaku Matsuda, whose sardonic, hyperkinetic Sato is the film's primary antagonist. Scott recalls that despite the outrageous villainy he unleashed in *Rain*, Matsuda 'was essentially a comedian, known for a very amusing television series [Matsuda also was a film actor who appeared in his first Japanese motion picture in 1973]. Yusaku, I think, was also a bit of an icon with the female population. Anyway, he was very popular in Japan. What was he personally like? A sweetheart. Really a nice guy.'

One would never know this from his appearance in *Black Rain*, however, since Matsuda (who sadly died of bladder cancer on 6 November 1989, not long after *Black Rain*'s American release) portrays Sato as a villain favouring the outrageous and the extreme. Sato's weapon of choice is the blade; he decapitates Charlie Vincent, slices up the *yakuza* competition, and later cuts off his own finger (during a scene that had originally featured a shot of Sato's severed digit, which was then edited out of the film). And Sato performs these appalling acts with a sardonic and gleeful intensity, making *Black Rain* one of Scott's most violent films.

Such a circumstance seems a logical point to pause for a moment and question Scott about his own views on violence. 'Everyone knew *Black Rain* was going to be a bit more violent than most of my films going in,' Scott says. 'But that was strictly a reflection of the script – I'm not obsessional about this topic. But if you want my thoughts on portraying screen violence… well, Francis Coppola does violence very well, you know. Francis's way is very economical. Very swift. Because of that, his violence is real and effective and there's no glamorous waltz before or afterwards. It's just death. I tend to adopt that style myself. That's how violence occurs in reality. It erupts, it's usually very brief, then it's "over".'

Though the violence in *Black Rain* may seem commonplace to those raised on Japanese samurai pictures, the manner in which Ridley Scott peppers his own 'Asian action' film with some interesting (if only glancing) social asides is not. *Black Rain* takes the audience on a tour of a contemporary Japan rarely seen in Western films; it is a society seething with corruption and mob violence, with prostitution and the repression of the individual, a divided country whose sleek city life is counterpointed by an archaic, quasi-feudal rural culture. The Japan of *Black Rain* also features an urban phenomenon rarely exposed in 1988–9, but increasingly commonplace today – homelessness.

In sum, then, if one were to watch only these moments (or the last hour of *Black Rain*, which is when it is most tightly paced), one might judge the film an above-average, perfectly acceptable bit of *noir* entertainment, a Hollywood action movie made deeper than its script because of the involvement of Ridley Scott. On the whole, however, *Black Rain* is hobbled by its negative aspects. The film is sometimes too predictable, for instance; also overlong, with an unconvincing subplot involving Douglas' tentative relationship with an American woman (Kate Capshaw, curiously irrelevant here), who works as a hostess in a Osakan karaoke bar.

In spite of its weaknesses, *Black Rain* did find favour with American audiences. The film grossed a respectable $45 million during its US initial run, and was considered a medium-sized hit. Many newspaper reviewers also praised *Rain* as an important comeback project in the career of Ridley Scott (who'd never gone away in the first place).

Ironically, Scott's true *coup de foudre* was to arrive two years later. This would take the form of a feminist 'buddy/road picture' named *Thelma and Louise*.

8 Two Girls and a Thunderbird

Callie Khouri, the author of *Thelma and Louise*, was born in San Antonio, Texas. After attending Purdue University to study acting and drama, Khouri relocated to Los Angeles, where she pursued more formal acting training. Khouri then worked at Propaganda Films (a trendy City of Angels music video/production house) producing rock videos for the likes of musicians Alice Cooper and Robert Cray, before turning to screenwriting.

Khouri hit upon the basic idea for *Thelma and Louise* one night as she sat outside her home in her parked car. What single event, Khouri wondered, could possibly force a woman to jettison her former conventional life in favour of a completely unconventional one? The situation Khouri imagined (an attempted rape ending in murder) was then injected by the writer into a serio-comic road movie, with two female protagonists.

Thelma Dickinson is a naïve Arkansas housewife unhappily married to her childhood sweetheart, the obnoxious, chauvinistic Darryl. Thelma's best friend Louise Sawyer – outspoken, tough-minded, streetwise – is an older, unmarried coffee-shop waitress with her own problems, stuck as she is waiting on tables and waiting for a romantic commitment from Jimmy, Louise's decent but always-away musician boyfriend.

As *T & L* begins, Louise convinces Thelma to join her on a weekend trip to the mountains. Their transport will be Louise's prized possession, a 1966 Thunderbird convertible. But on the first night of their getaway, a drunken Thelma is almost raped outside a roadside honky-tonk by Harlan, a stranger Thelma had danced with inside the bar. Louise intervenes by shooting and killing the attacker. Certain that Harlan's death will be misinterpreted as a homicide, the women agree not to report the killing, and begin a cross-country flight to Mexico. However, that decision results in the pair being pursued by Hal Slocumbe, a sympathetic yet relentless police detective. And what began as a simple weekend getaway soon becomes an allegorical odyssey, as the increasingly empowered *Thelma and Louise* blaze a trail across the American Southwest in their vintage T-Bird, cathartically overcoming representatives of every negative male stereotype – domineering men, foul-mouthed men, violent men – until the two women are literally left with nowhere else to run.

Part parable, part road movie, part social commentary, part buddy film, *Thelma and Louise* is also, despite the gravity of the preceding synopsis, a comedy. The film's picaresque aspects, however, are subordinate to its serious subtext. For the supposedly comic escapades of *Thelma and Louise* are actually a string of social indictments, no-win situations the women must endure precisely because they are women.

Such a feminist declaration, needless to say, might seem an unusual project for the likes of Ridley Scott. But consider. Many of Scott's prior films had already featured strong, independent women – Diana Quick's passionate but practical mistress (*The Duellists*), Sigourney Weaver's indomitable Ripley (*Alien*), Daryl Hannah's lethal Pris (*Blade Runner*). So perhaps one should not be too surprised at Scott's acceptance of a project that, says the director, 'basically took apart the whole male species'.

But what of *Thelma and Louise*'s comedic slant? Comedy, after all, definitely was a genre previously unvisited by Ridley Scott. How did he deal with these elements of the film? More to the point, how did Khouri's script come to Scott's attention?

The director discovered *T & L* in mid-1990, roughly a year after the release of *Black Rain*. This was a period when Scott was again producing and directing commercials; at the same time, he was broadening the scope of the London-based RSA, which by 1990 was operating a Los Angeles branch office (this opened in 1986). 'I was also getting around to thinking what the hell I should do for the next feature film,' Scott adds.

That question was answered when Callie Khouri took her *T & L* script to Mimi Polk, Executive Vice President of Percy Main

Productions, the feature film development company Scott had started in 1980. 'Mimi had been with me since *Legend*,' says Scott, 'which was the first time I'd had the beginnings of a very small development company. Mimi ran that. She basically was the first person to run any kind of development office for me. [Mimi Polk is listed as an Associate Producer on *Someone to Watch Over Me*. She is also credited as a full producer on *Thelma and Louise*, as an Executive Producer on *1492: Conquest of Paradise* (under the name 'Mimi Polk Sotela'), and as a full producer on *White Squall* (where she is listed as 'Mimi Polk Gitlin'). Polk left Scott Free, the development company that arose from Percy Main, in 1996. She is now an independent producer.]

'Anyway, before Callie Khouri brought *Thelma and Louise* to Mimi, she'd already taken the screenplay to a few other places with no luck. But Callie perceived Percy Main as a small company that might be more receptive to her material. She was on the money with that one. And her timing was good. I'd just started, in a serious way, to co-ordinate the build-up of Percy Main; I wanted to crank up the volume on the company. I also was looking for ways to expand my own development process so I wouldn't be stuck at the end of one movie without a new one to do. And I'd been searching for a char-acter-oriented script having very much to do with people.'

Once Polk had passed it on to the director, Scott agreed that Khouri's screenplay seemed to fit all of his requirements. 'Callie's script was very well planned. The structure was excellent, and the story itself was really good – dramatic, humorous, slightly mythi-cal in its proportions. *Thelma and Louise* was also about the truth. You rarely get scripts that are about the truth.'

When pressed to expand on that last comment, Scott says, 'I liked the way Callie's script put the male/female relationship into perspective. It was written so as maybe to make audiences recog-nize certain aspects of themselves while watching *Thelma and Louise*, things that they may or may not have wanted to keep after seeing the film. I also liked how Callie inverted the way movies sometimes stereotype women, since each of the eight guys in *Thelma and Louise* actually represented a different portion of one whole man. Most of those parts weren't under control, though. Some were pretty negative. That's not to say I ever felt that *Thelma and Louise* was anti-male or into male-bashing. Because it really wasn't. Although I do think it was one of those infrequent screenplays that honestly dealt with what a lot of women have to put up with.'

Surprisingly, although Scott was greatly impressed by Khouri's effort, he originally gave no thought to directing her script himself.

> I didn't think *Thelma* was for me to direct because I hadn't really been down this almost totally character-based route before; I also think Callie had never expected that I *would* direct it. So going in, I initially viewed the film as a serious attempt to say, 'Look – Percy Main can develop a good script, hire me to *produce* it, and then find a good director to shoot it.' But then I wound up interviewing various directors who were only curious about why I wasn't going to direct it. There were also some pretty weird comments. One person said, 'I've got a problem with the women. We'd have to rewrite that.' I told him, 'The whole point of *Thelma and Louise* is that you gotta have a problem with the women.' Another guy told me, 'I've got a problem with the men.' I said, 'You've gotta have a problem with the men, because those men are all of us.' Then there was the director who said, 'This is nothing. There's no story. It's just about two bitches in a convertible.' Finally, in exasperation, I thought, 'Well, fuck you all. *I'll* direct it.

Scott's decision to both direct and produce *Thelma and Louise* undoubtedly helped secure the film's financing. This was surprisingly minimal – *T & L* was made for only $16 million, with funding coming from MGM, Pathé Entertainment and United International Pictures. As for the film's key crew members, these were Adrian Biddle (Cinematographer), Thom Noble (Editor), and Production Designer Spencer Norris (who had served in the same capacity for *Black Rain*). Callie Khouri, meanwhile, and Dean O'Brien (who'd helped Khouri launch her script) signed on as Co-producers. Polk and Scott took on the film's full producing chores, while Hans Zimmer, composer for *Black Rain*, was hired to create *Thelma and Louise*'s original music.

Significantly, *T & L* marked the first time the music track of a Ridley Scott film reflected an industry trend that had been more or less inspired by 1973's *American Graffiti*; that is, peppering the majority of a film's soundtrack with pre-existing rock songs. Unlike some other directors, however, Scott (who has always worked closely with his composers) took a hands-on approach and selected *T & L*'s songs himself. These most notably included Marianne Faithfull's

'The Ballad of Lucy Jordan' and Toni Childs' 'House of Hope'.

Principal photography for *Thelma and Louise* began on 11 June 1990. By then, Scott had decided that none of the film would be shot in a studio. Instead, *T & L* was filmed entirely on location.

This, Scott told the *Thelma and Louise* presskit, was 'a distinct advantage. There are a lot of things that Americans live with that they never really see, because they are such a part of their culture, because these things are so ingrained in their lives. As an "outsider", however, I can drive around the desert Southwest and get excited about miles and miles of telephone poles, telephone poles that the average American might just take for granted.'

Among the 54 locations used by *Thelma and Louise* – none situated in Arkansas – were areas in and around Los Angeles. These included Thousand Oaks, whose locally famous DuPar's Restaurant served as the coffee shop where Louise works as a waitress; Tarzana, where Thelma's tree-lined 'Arkansas' neighbourhood was shot; and the Silver Bullet Saloon in Long Beach, which doubled as the bar where Thelma meets Harlan and does a raucous country-and-western line dance called the 'Tush Push' (filmed with 250 extras).

Gorman, California, then served as a primary out-of-LA location for *Thelma and Louise*. So did Utah's Arches National Park and Canyonlands National Park (also in Utah), which stood in, respectively, for Arizona and New Mexico. 'We shot a lot around Bakersfield (California) too, like where you see the women driving past the farmlands,' adds Scott. 'We filmed the crop-dusting plane buzzing the T-Bird in the San Joaquin Valley. That wasn't planned, by the way. We got out to the location, I saw this plane dusting crops nearby, and I sent over an assistant to offer the pilot 200 bucks to see if he'd do a bit of flying for us. He said, "Sure!"'

Principal photography for *Thelma and Louise* took about 12 weeks and wrapped on 31 August 1990, making it a relatively quick 'shoot'. Of course, Scott needed the proper performers to work with during this period. And since *T & L* still remains the most character-driven Scott film, it now seems only proper to devote a bit more space than usual in this book to explore the actors and circumstances behind those characters.

Scott first cast the film's two leads. This was done with an eye towards acquiring female performers who not only possessed proven acting skills, but personal, inner strengths as well. To this end Scott chose Susan Sarandon (for Louise), an actor whose first film had been *Joe* (1970); Sarandon had also scored good critical notices for her work on *The Rocky Horror Picture Show* (1975), *Pretty Baby* (1978) and *The Hunger* (directed by Tony Scott, 1983). For Thelma, Scott cast Geena Davis. Davis made her feature debut in *Tootsie* (1982) and then delivered a bravura performance for David Cronenberg's remake of *The Fly* (1986) before winning the 1988 Best Supporting Actress Oscar for her work in *The Accidental Tourist*.

We went round a little bit with the studio at first trying to decide who'd be the best *Thelma and Louise* [Scott recalls]. So I talked to two or three big female stars. But I didn't feel they were appropriate. I wanted the film to have a certain pseudo-documentary reality, and I felt audiences might have had trouble accepting super high-profile actresses in reality-based roles.

Now, at the time Geena Davis wasn't that big a star. I'd always been impressed by her talent, though. Geena's a dramatist with a genuine comedic gift. A true original, very inventive and quite fascinating, one of those actors who changes with the role. She's not at all like Thelma, either, not a ditz. Geena's actually highly intelligent. And she was also already aware of Callie's script. In fact, a few actresses were. Because once a script is identified by a director putting his handle on it, you'd be amazed how fast that information gets out and is covered by all the agencies, who then send the screenplay to the relevant actors.

Anyway, when Geena heard I was going to direct *Thelma and Louise*, she tracked things very quickly, came in, and saw me on her own. Geena basically pitched us for the part. She said, 'I want do this; I just want you to know that.' So I picked her first.

As for Susan... well, Susan Sarandon has had such a dignified growth as an actress. She's always inventive, continually surprising, and very funny! In fact, Susan's one of the best actresses we've got. And I thought she'd be the best pairing with Geena. I wanted Louise to be like Thelma's older sister, and Susan has this definite note of natural authority. So we cast Susan second. She and Geena got on like gangbusters. They genuinely enjoyed working with one another. I think you can see that in the film. [Susan Sarandon and Geena Davis also enjoyed working with Ridley Scott. Early on, in fact, the director was given an affectionate nickname by these women – both took to calling Scott 'Bo', or 'Bo Ridley'.]

Casting the proper men for *Thelma and Louise* was, of course, just as important as finding the right women. Chief among these masculine roles was Hal Slocumbe, the warm-hearted police detective who senses that there's more to *Thelma and Louise*'s lawless escapades than meets the eye. For this critical part (the only completely sympathetic, if not totally believable, male in the film) Scott cast Harvey Keitel, who, since *The Duellists*, had been elevated from his previous status as a reliable character performer into the select circle of America's finest actors.

As for the part of Darryl Dickinson, Thelma's petulant, childishly self-important husband, Scott chose Christopher McDonald (previously seen in *Outrageous Fortune, Grease 2* and *Chances Are*). McDonald had been recommended by Geena Davis. As the director recalls, Davis told him that McDonald was 'a friend, and very talented, and that I must meet him. So I said OK. But Chris didn't look like a jerk when he walked in for his reading – he's actually a fairly handsome kind of character. It quickly became pretty apparent, though, that in real life Chris was funnier than shit. For example, during his scenes with Harvey Keitel, Harvey could hardly speak without laughing, because Chris was always doing these hilarious things just before the camera rolled.'

Despite his humorous qualities, Darryl veers dangerously close to a buffoonish caricature of the smothering husband (just as the crude, leering truck driver – whose 18-wheeler is ultimately blown up by the two women – seems a grotesque stereotyping of the sex-obsessed working man). Darryl's saving grace, however, is that he is completely unaware of his own foolishness. Consequently, the actions of Thelma's husband – which would be intolerable in the real world – became, through McDonald's comic performance, at least bearable in *Thelma and Louise*'s fictional universe.

'The thought had passed through my mind that we might be going a little far with the burlesque side of Darryl,' observes Scott. 'In fact, I hadn't initially planned to go that far with either Darryl or the truck driver. But as things progressed, those performances were working out comedically. I thought, "Well, it's taking this form anyway. So if nothing else, at least *Thelma and Louise* will be comic." And comedy is king, right? So at least the film will get more attention because of that, and therefore, more people will see it. Which of course is also the target. But I basically decided to portray some of the men comedically because, if they couldn't be sympathetic, at least they'd be amusing. And don't forget – Chris was playing the archetypal jerk husband. Any laughs he got helped humanize him.'

Actually, it was one moment of Christopher McDonald's performance that made Scott decide to expand the parodistic aspects of Darryl and the trucker.

'You know that scene where Darryl comes rushing out of his house to get into his car, and he slips and falls and gets a big laugh?' asks Scott. 'Well, that happened during the first day of shooting. It was an accident. Everybody on the crew burst out laughing. But I was trying to say "Shut the fuck up!" because we'd left the camera running. Fortunately, Chris is quick on his feet. He recovered, got in the car, and drove off. Later on, I figured that that moment was a good clue as to how many people are kind of ridiculous in real life. So I decided to up the ante on Darryl, and the truck driver, a little bit after that.'

One final footnote regarding Christopher McDonald involves his off-screen relationship with Geena Davis. Prior to their appearing as husband and wife on *Thelma and Louise*, Davis and McDonald had actually been engaged in real life! In fact, the couple had gone so far as to complete their wedding rehearsals, before finally (and amicably) calling the marriage off.

Marriage, or at least the potential for it, also underlies the relationship between Louise and Jimmy. As previously noted, Jimmy is an itinerant musician and 'significant other' in Louise's life. He was played by Michael Madsen (brother of actress Virginia Madsen), a hulking, sleepy-eyed performer whose screen debut came in 1983 with *War Games*. Madsen later achieved movie immortality through the notorious 'ear-slicing' scene in the 1992 *Reservoir Dogs*; prior to *T & L*, he had also garnered small roles in films like *The Natural* (*1984*) and *The Doors* (1991).

'I liked Michael's look,' Scott replies, when asked why Madsen was cast for the part of a man whose hesitation to commit terminates his relationship with Louise. 'Sometimes I can go very much on just what a performer looks like as they walk in the room, even before they speak. So when Michael came in I thought, "Hmm, this guy's really interesting. He's got a kind of slightly tough, even violent sort of look to him, yet there's something appealing as well." After we spoke, I realized Michael had a *lot* of interesting qualities. One was this touch of, if not exactly Elvis Presley, then Eddie Cochran, you know? Michael's definitely got that arse-kicking rock 'n' roll thing.'

However, as much as *T & L* would enhance Madsen's professional standing, it was actor Brad Pitt who received the greatest career boost from *Thelma and Louise*. Born 18 December 1963 in Shawnee, Oklahoma, Pitt, like Madsen, was not a complete acting neophyte prior to his breakthrough in Scott's film. However, the blonde, vaguely Robert Redford-ish performer had only secured small roles in the likes of *Less Than Zero* (1989), or appeared in small films such as *Cutting Class* (also 1989), *Too Young To Die?* (1990) and *Johnny Suede* (1991). Therefore, Pitt was still very much an 'unknown' before working with Ridley Scott on *Thelma and Louise*.

Yet the young performer's portrayal of sexy cowboy 'JD' – a handsome and mysterious hitchhiker whose backside Thelma takes an immediate 'likin' to' after she and Thelma pick him up on the highway – would prove a launching pad for Pitt's present-day career.

We looked at a lot of actors for the part of JD [Scott says], then got down to about three. But Brad was already potentially what he was going to become, so we went with him. He had an energy and freshness that was very appealing. That was important, because JD was a catalyst in the film. I mean, the sexual relationship between Brad and Geena, them having this crazy romp in a motel while Susan and Michael are breaking off their relationship in another room – that was one of the things I'd really liked about Callie's script. To have that scene and then have Thelma tell Louise about this wonderful new experience, only to find that JD's stolen all their money as soon as Thelma's back was turned, was another great moment. And of course after Louise realizes they've been robbed, she sort of caves in emotionally. Thelma takes control and becomes the strong one. So JD is directly responsible, among other things, for the way the women almost mystically switch personalities. Brad did a great job with all that.

J.D, Jimmy and Darryl are the romantic focuses of *Thelma and Louise*, but a clutch of lesser men also influence the narrative. Among them are a rigidly authoritarian state trooper (Jason Beghe), whom Thelma locks in the trunk of his own police cruiser, and a dreadlocked mountain bike rider (Noel Walcott), who discovers the trapped trooper – only to blow marijuana smoke through the bullet holes perforating the cruiser's trunk lid ('That's a funny bit,' notes Scott. 'Sort of a perverse moment of poetic justice'). The smooth, seemingly harmless Harlan, Thelma's would-be rapist, was played by Timothy Carhart, a stage actor who worked in New York and Los Angeles and had previously appeared in such television programmes as the 1989 CBS television series *Island Son* and feature films like *Working Girl* (1988), *Pink Cadillac* (1989) and *The Hunt for Red October* (1990).

> The attempted rape was tricky in a lot of ways [says Scott]. The most difficult thing was to find the right actor to play Harlan. We had to have a guy who was attractive and charming, because Thelma really enjoys dancing with him before they leave the club. But we also needed someone who could convey just the right mixture of disbelief and anger when Thelma refuses an encounter with him. You see, Harlan's wrong about that. He misreads Thelma totally. She doesn't want to have sex, and she tells him to stop. And when women say 'stop' you've gotta stop. That's why there's no justification for date rape. But Harlan doesn't stop. So Louise blows him away. Later on, it's suggested Louise was probably raped herself sometime earlier, in Texas, which she won't drive through. We never really nailed that down, exactly. But Louise's suggested rape at least explains why she kills Harlan *after* he's stopped attacking Thelma. Harlan was a thankless part, really. So [Carhart] and I talked about that scene fairly carefully. He was very effective.

Thelma and Louise's last significant male is the film's foul-mouthed trucker, an absurdly sexist character whose crude propositioning moves the two women to riddle the man's rig with bullets. For this short but memorable performance, Scott cast Marco St John. 'Funnily enough,' Scott says, 'that guy then went off and played Hamlet in Philadelphia a month after doing our movie. He wasn't anything like the trucker he played in *Thelma and Louise*. In fact, he kept telling me, "Jesus Christ! After this, I'll never get a date with another woman!"'

T & L's final key character is Louise's 1966 Thunderbird. This was represented by five identical convertibles - one 'principal' car, one back-up, one camera car, and two stunt vehicles. Each had been located by Terry Collis, *T & L*'s Transportation Co-ordinator. As many shots involving the T-Bird showed *Thelma and Louise* dri-

Thelma and Louise, **Scott's female buddy movie, was a success both critically and at the box office and is remembered by the director with affection, 'It was the best time I've had making a movie since my first film. I thoroughly enjoyed myself. I think everybody else had a wonderful time too.'**

ving down highways and backroads, Scott had a simple A-frame built on to the front of the principal Thunderbird's grille to act as a camera mount. The principal T-Bird was then filmed as it was towed behind another vehicle (the camera car was simply driven by the actors as their scenes were photographed from inside it). As for the low, impressive tracking shot that starts at the vehicle's front

bumper, glides down its side and stops at its rear tail-light – all
while the Thunderbird is moving – Scott filmed this himself, while
riding alongside the T-Bird in another vehicle. The director had to
lean out over the road for this shot, while an assistant prevented
him from tumbling on to the asphalt by holding on to his belt.

'Louise's car was always a T-Bird, right from Callie Khouri's first
draft,' Scott adds. 'I think Callie identified it as a car that's always
represented a symbol of freedom for her, because the Thunderbird
was one of the last great American cars. I mean, American automobiles used to have their own absolute singular identity that
somehow reflected everything that was attractive about the United
States. Now you see a Lincoln and it looks like a Honda Accord.'

The Thunderbird also figures prominently in the film's conclusion. By then the pair have been chased to the rim of a deep
canyon. Driver Louise pauses for a moment, unsure of how to deal
with the hordes of pursuing police cars which have chased them to
the cliff's edge. 'Let's keep going,' Thelma urges. Despite their
fear, both women smile in exultation, clasp hands, and rocket their
T-Bird over the cliff into the deep canyon beyond, as an errant
breeze wafts away a Polaroid of them smiling for the camera (ironically, this climactic double suicide underlines Khouri's ongoing
'no way out' subtext in the most pessimistic manner possible).

Three takes were filmed for *T & L*'s downbeat ending. Each time,
a separate Thunderbird was stripped of its engine, mounted on a
hidden ramp installed near the edge of a gorge in southern Utah (at
whose bottom was a swiftly-flowing river), and detailed with two
Thelma and Louise dummies. A metal cable was then attached to
the convertible, run through a '2-to-1' block-and-tackle system,
and tethered to an off-camera Jeep bearing a 600 horsepower
motor. During filming, the Jeep quickly accelerated to a speed of
45 mph – the '2-to-1' system doubled the speed of the cable running through it and pulled the Thunderbird over the cliff at 90
mph. Overcranking then gave a 'floating' quality to the shot.

'We ended up putting all three cars into the bloody drink so I
could choose a take I liked,' Scott recalls. 'It was quite tricky, that
shot. But it was pretty well done.'

Scott actually filmed a slightly extended version of *Thelma and
Louise*'s ending that was later cut from theatrical prints (it does
appear on MGM's 1997 '*Thelma and Louise* Widescreen

Collector's Edition' laserdisc as a supplement). This original climax included footage of the T-Bird dropping down into the canyon,
reaction shots from Harvey Keitel (who could be seen looking into
the canyon with a sad expression on his face) at the women's
deaths, Keitel walking back towards the hordes of pursuing policemen (who were actual local law enforcement officials recruited for
the film), and, most importantly, a reprise of the same wide shot
that opens *Thelma and Louise*. This image was of an empty dirt
road leading to a distant, sun-kissed mountain. ('I put in that shot
of the mountain and deserted road at the beginning of *T & L* as sort
of a visual metaphor,' says the director. 'It suggested the freedom
these women were after.') In Scott's 'alternate ending', however,
this road was occupied by Louise's Thunderbird, which could be
seen motoring away from the viewer towards the distant peak, as a
cloud of dust trailed behind it. At the same time, blues legend BB
King sang 'Better Not Look Down' on the soundtrack.

> The original ending worked well enough [explains the director]. But then I real-
> ized it undercut the emotion of *Thelma and Louise*'s final gesture somehow.
> That additional footage diminished the nobility of their decision to stay free
> and drive over the edge. Some people were also upset by the fact that when
> you saw their car falling down into the canyon, it made it hard to escape the
> fact that the women were dead. So I cut the original conclusion back a bit,
> ending on a freeze-frame of their car taking off into space. And early on,
> there'd also been some anxiety about Callie's ending in general. 'Not from me
> – I thought it was a pretty good one. But I'm always open to something bet-
> ter. Nobody came up with anything, though. Anyway, I liked the reality of them
> having nowhere left to turn. And later, when we previewed the film, we got a
> lot of test cards saying, 'Whatever you do, do not change this ending! Not
> only is it the antithesis of a Hollywood ending, it's the *right* ending.'

Apparently so – *Thelma and Louise* was the surprise hit of the 1991
film season. It also bears repeated viewings, graced as it is by striking horizontal compositions and such evocative moments as the
hauntingly ambiguous scene of a much older woman totally unnerv-
ing Louise by silently looking at her with a dignified, yet unread-
able, stare. The film earned over three times its cost in the United
States alone, grossing $46 million in America. *T & L* then reaped
a 'Best Screenplay Written Directly for the Screen' Academy Award
for Callie Khouri in 1992; Davis and Sarandon were nominated for

Best Actress, Biddle for Best Cinematography, and Scott for Best Director. The film also became a 1991 *Time* magazine cover story, and ignited numerous debates, mostly among bewildered critics used to accusing Scott of being 'all style and no substance'.

Today, the names *Thelma and Louise* have entered into contemporary American folklore. But Scott himself personalizes the experience, looking back on the film with affection. '*T & L* was the best time I've had making a movie since my first film,' the director recalls. 'I thoroughly enjoyed myself. I think everybody else had a wonderful time too. And it went like lightning.'

Sources close to the production point out that *Thelma and Louise* also marked changes in the ways Scott shot a film, as well as his on-set demeanour. For instance, *T & L* was the first time Scott shot almost an entire feature with at least two cameras running simultaneously throughout, a technique which, explains the director, 'not only allows me to get multiple angles of the same shot, but really helps keep performances loose and spontaneous. I've used that technique ever since.' And then there is the personality issue. Previously Ridley Scott had sometimes been accused of adopting a chilly or off-putting manner while making his movies – a charge that this writer feels is actually a misinterpretation of Scott's natural English reserve, or of the way he brings both intense concentration and the utmost professionalism to his sets. 'But Ridley really relaxed during this project,' says an anonymous *T & L* co-worker. 'Maybe it was being surrounded by all those women. I really don't know. But making *Thelma and Louise* seemed to help Ridley let down his guard a bit.'

'On the whole,' the director himself responds, 'when I think back on *Thelma and Louise* now, I realize we really touched a nerve with that picture. But you know what I was happiest with? That we'd made a funny film. The politics really were secondary to that. I just enjoyed the hell out of making a comedy, and discovering that I could make it look good at the same time.'

9 A Man's World

After *Thelma and Louise*, Scott directed three other features (a fourth, *Gladiator*, had just started production as this book was being published). Unfortunately, none prompted the same excitement that greeted *T & L*; instead, each was referred to as an artistic and/or commercial disappointment during its original run.

Yet if this book has established nothing else, it is that Ridley Scott's films often contain more than meets the eye. The same principle holds true for *1492: Conquest of Paradise*, *White Squall* and *G.I. Jane*; these efforts may have received dismissive initial responses, but on closer examination they possess substantive cores and intriguing narratives. They also share a common theme – the high personal costs paid by outsiders willing to challenge the dominant social order. In *1492*, Christopher Columbus overcomes aristocratic arrogance and religious ignorance to prove the existence of a New World; his reward is scorn, imprisonment, and disgrace. *White Squall*'s Captain Sheldon teaches positive moral values to the young men in his charge; in return, Sheldon loses his ship, watches his wife drown, and is tried for criminal neglect. A US Senator convinces *G.I. Jane*'s Lt O'Neil that she can achieve better parity for her gender by becoming the first female Navy SEAL; O'Neil then endures horrific mental/physical abuse only to discover that the same Senator never expected her to succeed in the first place.

This is not to say that *1492*, *Squall* and *Jane* scale the same lofty heights reached in Scott's best work; as a whole, they do not. On the other hand, their primary faults are erratic rhythms and uneven structures, certainly not thin content or poor execution.

Unfortunately, only 45,000 words were allotted for this book. And like any soldier running low on ammunition, I must carefully choose my shots. This is why the preceding chapters of *Ridley Scott: The Making of His Movies* have been devoted to little-known biographical facts about the director's life, to his most popular films, and to his most unfairly neglected projects.

It is also why the relatively sparse overview that follows only touches upon Scott's latest works.

Following *Thelma and Louise*'s attention-grabbing release, Scott once again confounded viewer expectations by plunging into a lavish $47 million historical epic. This, his eighth feature, was titled *1492: Conquest of Paradise*.

Historically accurate, impressively researched, *1492* recounts the struggles of famed 15th-century navigator Christopher Columbus (who was born an Italian, but lived as an expatriate in Spain) to discover the New World. The film's ambitious screenplay was written by Roselyne Bosch. This young French journalist had travelled to Spain (in 1987) on a routine assignment for the French news weekly *Le Point*, in order to write an article on Spain's celebration of the 500th anniversary of Columbus's maiden voyage. However, Bosch was shocked to discover that approximately 40 million parchments pertaining to the period, plus scores of letters in Columbus's own handwriting, still existed in the provincial archives of Madrid and Seville. Galvanized by this incredible mass of material, Bosch wrote a script placing the Italian mariner's first two historic voyages in the context of the social, religious and political forces surrounding them. Her screenplay also touched upon Columbus's complex, often contradictory character, for the mariner Bosch had unearthed was a fearless visionary who was also an active (if reluctant) participant in the savage colonialism of the New World, a charismatic leader ultimately undone by his own stubbornness and pride.

In 1990, after failing to interest French producers in the project, Bosch and producer Alain Goldman brought the *1492* script to Ridley Scott (who had been coincidentally thinking of doing his own Columbus film). The director liked Bosch's story, and was attracted by its opportunity to recreate its 15th-century backgrounds. Scott then handpicked famed French performer Gérard

Dépardieu (*The Last Metro, Green Card*) to portray Columbus. 'I couldn't think of anyone else being that big, in terms of having the proper energy and outsized personality for the Columbus character,' Scott says.

Rounding off *1492*'s key cast were American performer Armand Assante (as Sanchez, the ambivalent courtier/banker who introduces Columbus to his royal patron, Queen Isabella of Spain), the fine Canadian actor Michael Wincott (as the dangerous, disdainful, marvellously named nobleman 'Noxica'), and Sigourney Weaver as Queen Isabella. (Scott originally wanted Anjelica Huston for this role, but her reluctance to commit eventually lead to Weaver's casting in the part.) Finances for *1492* – which, Scott says, 'was my first shot at a fully independent movie, with totally independent financing' – were then acquired by raising $10 million from Paramount (for American rights), $11 million from the French production company Gaumont (for French distribution rights), and by preselling *1492* on a territory-by-territory basis at the 1991 Cannes Film Festival.

1492's principal photography took place in four different countries on two different continents. Some interior sets were filmed at England's Pinewood Studios; the production also travelled to Spain, the Dominican Republic, and Costa Rica, where most of the jungle scenes involving Columbus's New World adventures were shot. Filming began on 2 December 1991, outside the Spanish town of Cáceres, in a 16th-century Spanish villa doubling for an ancient monastery named Santa Maria de la Rabida. Production then continued for 82 working days, and involved some 400 people.

A unexpected obstacle arose when *Superman* producers Alexander and Ilya Salkind announced that they too were doing a 'Columbus movie' named *Christopher Columbus: The Discovery*. Of course, two competing Columbus films ran the risk of severely undercutting each other's profits, and distributors, attorneys and cinema chains soon began arguing over various aspects of the two productions.

'Even with that aggravation, shooting *1492* went pretty well,' Scott says today. 'I tried to ignore the other film and just got on with it. And I actually enjoyed myself – I mean, how often does one get the chance to find working replicas of the *Nina*, the *Pinta* and the

Santa Maria?'

Two of these ships (the *Pinta* and the *Santa Maria*) were built by the production after Scott discovered suitable hulls in a boatyard in Bristol, England; *Paradise* Production Designer Norris Spencer then leased a *Nina* that had already been constructed by a '1492 Society', in Brazil.

Besides its famous ships, *1492* features an astonishing recreation of other late-15th-century artefacts. For example, La Isabella, the village Columbus established on the island of 'Hispaniola' (now known as Haiti and the Dominican Republic), was built near the Costa Rican coast 'around a magnificent tree I'd spotted during a location hunt'. This detailed set was equipped with a manor house for Columbus, a walled compound, a Spanish church sporting a 90-foot bell tower, and many other structures.

But *1492* is more than impressive sets – it also features brilliant set pieces. As Scott explains, one involved 'Columbus sitting on the deck of his ship at night during the first voyage, idly crushing an insect in his hand. Then he realizes what the hell it is – a land-based bug – and he turns around to see millions of such insects swarming around his lights. He's reached the New World. It's right in front of his face, but he can't see it, because it's night. I'd got the idea for that one evening when I was staring at some lights at our Costa Rica location. Insects twice the size of my two thumbs were kamikaze-ing into the bulbs, and I realized that land bugs would have been attracted to the lights on Columbus's ships, too.'

Other *1492* highlights include the explorer's first daylight glimpse of the New World. This magical moment was staged by a creating a fog bank from various 'smoke machines' mounted on land-based jeeps and offshore boats criss-crossing a Costa Rican beach; the fog was then blown away, slowly revealing the verdant jungle beneath. Scott also created perhaps the most authentic cannibal village ever committed to celluloid, and there is a short but significant shot of two rivers swirling into one another – one clear, one darkened with mud – that can be interpreted as a visual symbol for the 'muddying' influence of European culture on the New World's 'pure' native population.

Yet despite these and other accomplishments, after the film was released to American theatres on 2 October 1992 (one week before the Columbus Day holiday weekend), *1492* generated very little

heat, earning only $7.2 million during its US run (overseas gross-
es totalled $52 million). Some *1492* theorists opine that this dis-
mal response was due to American audiences having difficulty
understanding Dépardieu's French accent; others speculated that
those same Americans were simply bored by the complex politics.
Scott himself hypothesizes that 'having a competitive project come
out ahead of us didn't help [the Salkind's *Columbus* was released
in late August 1992]. And while I have great respect for Stanley
Jaffe, [then head of Paramount] who was courageous enough to take
a gamble on *1492*, I think Paramount's promotional department
just couldn't get hold of the picture.'

Another reason behind *1492*'s low key reception may have been
its initially slow pacing and general structuring. The film's first act
is rather ponderous, while its last half-hour has a rushed, disjointed feel, leading to a muted, emotionally unsatisfying climax. This
leaves only the film's second act, which is beautifully paced. In
fact, if one skips the film's initial half-hour altogether and enters
into the story just as Columbus is embarking upon his first voyage
(a simple enough programming trick on DVD or laserdisc players),
one subsequently encounters a riveting, very satisfying experience
indeed.

'Maybe I should have released a three-hour version of *1492*'
Scott says. 'We did have a three-hour cut and, contrary to popular
opinion, sometimes longer is better. But I recently watched *1492*
again on laserdisc, and I think it's a pretty good movie. I also think
it wasn't what people expected.'

With *1492* behind him, Scott and brother Tony forged a multi-pic-
ture deal with 20th Century Fox. Ridley's first proposed project
under this new arrangement was based on 'Crisis in the Hot Zone',
an October 1992 *New Yorker* article written by Richard Preston,
who later expanded his piece into a best-selling 1994 book.

'The Hot Zone' detailed the frightening true story of the discovery of the deadly tropical 'Ebola' filovirus, a disease which has an
incubation period of only one week and kills by virtually liquefy-
ing its hosts' internal systems. It was discovered at a Primate
Quarantine Unit in Reston, Virginia (located only 10 miles away
from Washington, DC), after US Veterinary Corps scientists there
realized that their test monkeys were dying from suspicious symp-

toms at an alarming rate – and that the microscopic cause of their deaths had contaminated the facility.

'The "Hot Zone" article seemed an excellent opportunity for me to develop a science-fact thriller,' notes Scott. 'So the rights were bought, Lynda Obst signed on as a producer, and Jodie Foster agreed to star [as real-life "Zone" protagonist Nancy Jaax]. We also got a very good script from James V. Hart.'

But Scott's *Hot Zone* soon encountered difficulties. Producer Arnold Kopelson, who'd unsuccessfully tried to secure the rights to Preston's *New Yorker* piece, decided instead to launch his own *fictional* Ebola project. This was titled *Outbreak*. A Warner Brothers production directed by Wolfgang Peterson, *Outbreak*, like *Christopher Columbus: The Discovery* before it, was put into production at the same time as Scott's own effort, again forcing the English director to contend with a competing film on the same subject. To further complicate matters, once megastar Robert Redford joined the *Hot Zone* cast as its male lead, he also brought along his own screenwriters, reportedly to make Redford's part larger than Jodie Foster's. This kicked off an internal power struggle, and Foster and Redford eventually bowed out of the film. Fox responded by killing the project.

Not being able to get the *Hot Zone* going was 'frustrating'. Scott adds. 'I would have loved to work with Jodie. I also thought it was one of those rare projects, like *Thelma and Louise*, that was actually about something.'

Yet other Scott Free projects did complete production during this period. One was *Monkey Trouble* (produced by Mimi Polk, executive produced by Scott), a charming 1994 film about a nine-year-old girl and her pet monkey. 1994 also saw Scott Free unveil a remake of a 1951 English film, *The Browning Version*, which originally featured Sir Michael Redgrave as a failed, middle-aged schoolteacher with an unfaithful wife. Director Mike Figgis's 1994 variant (with Scott for the first time 'acting as a hands-on feature producer') starred Albert Finney.

1995 then saw the Scott brothers become studio bosses. They achieved this career leap by heading up a consortium which paid $19.5 million to purchase Shepperton Studios, one of Europe's largest film-making facilities.

'I'd been coming to Shepperton for 25 years,' Scott says, 'and I was one of their best customers. So I knew the place very well. I also had a soft spot in my heart for it, because Shepperton was where I shot my first real studio movie (*Alien*). We've since done a lot of upgrading to the place.'

Still, Scott's added responsibilities as a studio executive did not quench his desire to direct another motion picture. Therefore, shortly before Christmas of 1994, the film-maker acquired a script by first-time screenwriter Todd Robinson entitled *White Squall*.

Squall related true events that occurred in 1961. These involved the *Albatross*, a square-rigged Brigantine ship housing The Ocean Academy, a 'floating prep school' for wealthy but troubled teenage boys. Thirteen of these young men (including Charles Gieg Jr) were embarked upon a routine voyage through the Caribbean when their craft was unexpectedly hit by a freak weather condition called a 'white squall'. This short but vicious storm which, acting like a lateral microburst, capsized and sank the ship, and four students and two faculty members were dragged down with it. The *Albatross*'s captain, Christopher Sheldon, was then tried for (but later acquitted of) criminal negligence.

Scott read *White Squall* exactly one day after the *Hot Zone* project fell apart. 'Losing *The Hot Zone* had been a little traumatic because I was so passionate about it,' the director continues. 'I'd also become anxious to prove that our production company could kick in another movie fairly quickly. So I looked around and found two pieces of material. One was called *Mulholland Falls* [a Forties-based thriller ultimately directed by Lee Tamahori in 1996]. The other was *White Squall*. I chose *Squall* because the more I thought about it, the more I realized that Robinson's script showed the *Albatross boys* making a difficult transition into manhood in a very unusual way. Their rite-of-passage story had been approached very earnestly – there was almost an ingenuous note to it – but [Robinson] had also recounted what Chuck Gieg went through with absolute honesty, and without being sentimental. I responded very well to that.'

White Squall's financing involved Largo Entertainment, Hollywood Pictures (a subsidiary of the Disney group) and Scott's production company. (Previously called 'Percy Main', by now it was 'Scott Free'. This is the banner under which Ridley and Tony Scott, Scott Free's other major partner, develop their own projects today.)

Between these entities, approximately $36 million was raised for the picture's budget. Next came the casting process.

To portray the tough-but-fair Captain Sheldon, Scott picked Jeff Bridges (*The Last Picture Show*). 'I think Jeff's one of the best actors in America,' Scott declares. 'A real artist. What's really remarkable about him is that Jeff somehow always finds a unique character in each piece he does.'

Although Bridges portrayed the principal adult in the film, *White Squall*'s main character focus was on the young Charles Gieg. Therefore, Scott first chose Scott Wolf (star of the Fox television series *Party of Five*) to play Gieg, followed by *Studio 54*/*Cruel Intentions* star Ryan Phillipe (whose shy Gil Martin suffers from a paralysing fear of heights), plus actors Jeremy Sisto (as Frank Beaumont) and Balthazar Getty (playing the bespectacled Tod Johnstone). Also cast were Catherine Goodall as Alice Sheldon, Captain Sheldon's physician wife, and the ever eccentric John (*The Deer Hunter*) Savage as Mr McCrea, the Ocean Academy's poetry-spouting English teacher.

White Squall crew members of note included: Producers Mimi Polk Gitlin and Rocky Lang; Cinematographer Hugh Johnson (a former business associate of *Alien* DP Derek Van Lynt, Johnson also worked as a camera assistant on *The Duellists* and directed *1492*'s second unit); Production Designers Peter J. Hampton and Leslie Tomkins; and Film Editor Gerry Hambling. Composer Jeff Rona then contributed *White Squall*'s wistful, eminently collectable score.

Viewed from one angle, *White Squall* can be seen as a distaff version of *Thelma and Louise*. Both films involve same-sex companions embarked upon picaresque trips, outer journeys mirrored by life-altering inner ones. Each production also particularizes the vehicles used for these trips. For *Thelma and Louise*, this was a 1966 Thunderbird; for *White Squall*, a 110-foot-long topsail schooner (built in West Germany) called *Eye of the Wind*. Owned by a New Zealander named Captain Tiger Timbs, the *Eye of the Wind* had already appeared in previous films such as *The Blue Lagoon* (1980) and *Taipan* (1986) before Ridley Scott used it to stand in for the *Albatross*.

With cast, crew and sailing ship secured, Scott next scouted appropriate locations for the film's principal photography phase (which occurred throughout mid-1995). Various bits of *White Squall* action were shot in Georgia, South Carolina and the Bahamas, but the bulk of the production was filmed in the West Indies. These southern Caribbean locations included the islands of St Lucia, St Vincent (whose spectacular volcanic lake appears near the end of *Squall*), and Grenada (which had last hosted a motion picture company in 1957, for *Island in the Sun*). An early sequence showing the *Albatross* encountering heavy, 40-foot high seas was then shot near the Cape of Good Hope, situated near the southern-most tip of Africa.

'The most difficult thing about doing *White Squall* was finding locations that hadn't been ruined by the cruise lines,' Scott says. 'Because where you find cruise ships, that's the beginning of the end – beautiful areas that used to have untouched towns and har-bours [now] are filled with new condominiums and posh Yves St Laurent shops.'

For the climactic squall itself, Scott originally hoped to shoot at least part of a *real* storm at sea. But this plan was abandoned when the production was unable to find a fittingly violent tempest. Scott next decided to stage *Squall*'s titled tempest (and the sinking of the *Albatross*) under more controllable conditions at the Mediterranean Film Studios. This cinematic facility is located in the town of Kalkara, on the island of Malta.

'According to the real Captain Sheldon [who, along with C. Gieg, served as a technical advisor], the genuine white squall had been like a gigantic downdraft,' Scott explains. 'It just sprang out of nowhere, hit the water, and created a kind of strange flattening effect. Like the opposite of a tidal wave. Then it hit the *Albatross*. Its sails immediately filled out and – bang! – the wind took the ship right over.'

Scott spent four weeks of the film's entire 14-week shooting schedule replicating this disaster at the Mediterranean Film Studios. The actual flipping over of the *Albatross* – which Scott recalls as being 'really hard work' – was accomplished through a combination of miniature vessels and full-scale sets. These latter were shot within the Mediterranean Film Studios' most famous asset, its enormous (exterior) watertank. This gigantic pool had already been utilized for waterlogged sequences in films such as *Popeye* (1980) and *Clash of the Titans* (1981). For *White Squall*, a full-scale, fully rigged recreation of the *Albatross*'s upper deck was first placed in the flooded tank, then fixed on to articulated metal platforms. These submerged supports rocked the bogus brigantine back and forth before tipping it over into the water-filled tank. Hundreds of thousands of gallons of sea water were simultaneously dropped on to the actors by large metal chutes, while overhead sprinklers and enormous wind machines blasted down on Scott's staged action, resulting in a very convincing maritime tragedy.

Other *White Squall* effects included an amazingly lifelike mechanical dolphin, which Sheldon clubs to death after one of his 'boys' heartlessly harpoons it. This creature was built by Edge Innovations, a Silicon Valley-based company dedicated to the creation of sophisticated animatronic creatures (the same company was responsible for the full-scale mechanical killer whales used in the 1993 *Free Willy*). The film also featured convincing digital 'squall F/X' by Ken Houston, of the British effects company Peerless Optical, who supplied a shot of computer-generated rain moving *horizontally* over the face of the ocean and impacting into the camera lens as well as a beautiful, otherworldly shot of a lightning bolt striking the sea's surface and creating a patch of boiling water.

Today Ridley Scott looks back with pleasure at the making of the film: 'When you do certain films like *Thelma and Louise* or *White Squall*, they happen so fast and are over so quickly you can't believe you actually shot them. The whole *Squall* experience was entirely wonderful, really – it was like taking a holiday.'

Yet any enjoyment Scott might have felt while making *White Squall* was surely offset by its poor reception at the American box-office. Following its US release (on 2 February 1996), the film grossed only $10.3 million; world-wide, it earned $40 million. American audiences were apparently put off by the film's leisurely pace, while some US critics attacked the necessity of the film's ending, which has Sheldon hauled before a maritime review board on charges of criminal negligence.

Possibly, those critics were right – *Squall*'s coda is dramatically unnecessary (and too long). Since the film's primary point is the young *Albatross* crew's journey into manhood, the sinking of their ship is a satisfying if sombre close to that journey, which by the climactic storm sequence has already charted the ethical/emotional

On the set of White Squall with Jeff Bridges (right). Over the years, Scott has managed to cast his films with some of the most talented actors around. 'I think Jeff is one of the best actors in America. A real artist.'

growth of Gieg and his companions. Whatever its flaws, however, *White Squall* does demonstrate a certain lyricism and sweetness not always present in Scott's other works. Moreover, in powerful sequences like the death of Sheldon's wife or the drowning of Ryan Phillippe (both of whom are trapped below decks as the *Albatross* sinks), *Squall* achieves a stark poignancy. The film's exceptional recreation of the overall feel of the early 1960s – an unrushed, polite world on the verge of the Cuban missile crisis, JFK's assassination, and the tragedy of Vietnam – is also remarkably authoritative. 'I think we did a good job of replicating the look and innocence of the early Sixties without sentimentalizing the period,' the director agrees.

Unfortunately, *White Squall* today has, like the *Albatross* before it, sunk without a trace. Still, Scott feels that his ninth feature at least accomplished one of his aims.

'At the end of the day,' the director says, 'I wanted the film to be cathartic to the survivors of the real *Albatross* disaster. I mean, I don't think those people ever had the chance to see their story told properly. I hope *White Squall* proved helpful in that respect.'

If Scott had been partially attracted to *White Squall* (and *1492*) because of its seafaring background (a maritime milieu the director knew from his father's business concerns), then *G.I. Jane* surely must have appealed to the Ridley Scott who'd once thought of enlisting in the British military. 'Don't forget that at one point in my life I almost joined the [Royal] Marines,' Scott says. 'So when *G.I. Jane* appeared I was curious about the military subculture it took place in.'

Scott's tenth film was based on an original screenplay by Danielle Alexandra, a 20th Century Fox executive and novelist (*China Doll, White Blood*) who had written *Jane* in response to the then current political debate concerning the issue of women serving in combat. Alexandra's script focused on Navy Lt Jordan O'Neil, a gifted female officer. Through the intervention of powerful US Senator Lillian DeHaven, O'Neil becomes the first woman to enlist in the Navy SEALs, an ultra-elite commando outfit whose training programme has a 60 per cent drop-out rate. *Jane* then followed O'Neil's struggles to complete this gruelling instruction period, and her fight to win the respect of O'Neil's hardbitten drill instructor, Master Chief John Urgayle.

Danielle Alexandra had specifically written the role of Jordan O'Neil for Demi Moore (*Ghost, Indecent Proposal, Disclosure*); Moore herself, as Scott recalls, 'then approached me to direct *Jane*. Actually, I'd met Demi on a couple of prior occasions, where we'd swapped ideas that didn't work out. But when Demi later came back and asked me if I wanted to do *G.I. Jane* with her, this time I said yes. Apart from *Jane*'s military angle, I'd always wanted to work with Demi, and I liked the fact that the subject-matter of *Jane* was so provocative. A woman entering combat training in a very rarefied area of the military, and how she fares against the obstacles placed in her way, seemed a challenging topic.'

The deal to put *G.I. Jane* into production included Hollywood Pictures, Largo Entertainment, Moving Pictures (Moore's production company), Caravan Pictures and Scott Free. A budget was set at $50 million, and 15 weeks of shooting scheduled throughout early 1997. In addition to Roger Birnbaum, Demi Moore, Suzanne Todd and Ridley Scott (all of whom received a Producer credit on *Jane*), the film's main crew consisted of Hugh Johnson (Cinematography), Pietro Scalia (Film Editing), Trevor Jones (Original Music), and Production Designer Arthur Max (who had previously designed some of Scott's television commercials).

'After Demi, my two major casting concerns were Senator DeHaven and Master Chief Urgayle,' Scott continues. 'I picked Anne Bancroft (*The Miracle Worker, The Elephant Man*) for the Senator because, frankly, to me she already seemed like one – Anne's a very incisive, smart and elegant woman. I decided to go a little against the grain for Urgayle, though, because I didn't want whoever took that role to be your typical Navy Chief. So I went with Viggo Mortensen (*Portrait of a Lady, Daylight, Carlito's Way*), who'd I'd been very impressed with after seeing him in a film called *The Indian Runner* (1991). Viggo's character there had exhibited a certain strength which was offbeat – and because it was offbeat, it was quite threatening, which I wanted Chief Urgayle to be.'

However, Scott also envisioned the forbidding Urgayle to be something more than a walking Buck knife. 'I saw Urgayle as dedicated and intelligent, too. He's not just macho. Urgayle genuinely believes that the SEALs are only as strong as the weakest link in their chain, and he treats O'Neil harshly because Urgayle's not

quite sure Demi isn't that link. That's why I was excited when
Viggo came up with the idea of Urgayle quoting [the] poetry [of
D.H. Lawrence and Pablo Neruda] during the SEAL training ses-
sions – it suggested other dimensions in the man.'

Yet once *G.I. Jane*'s casting was out of the way, another obstacle
presented itself. 'We were trying to get the co-operation of the Navy
and the Department of Defense for the film,' Scott says. 'But
although they did go into extensive talks with us and were very
curious about *G.I. Jane* at first, they also said there were certain
things about the script we'd have to change. Some of those were
puzzling – for instance, they told us that Naval officers didn't
swear. Then, it later became clear that the Navy and DOD didn't
want this film to happen.'

Perhaps the Naval hierarchy had been upset by *Jane*'s improper
terminology, since the term 'GI' (derivation: 'Government Issue') is
an Army designation, not a Naval one. In any event, the Navy eventually issued a statement objecting to the overall tone of *G.I. Jane*,
and refused to co-operate with its makers. *Jane*'s well-known leading lady attempted to have this refusal reversed by personally calling the Clinton White House in late 1996, during which time she
also pleaded for access to real Naval training facilities and military
equipment. However, she was turned down.

'We then decided to do it our own way,' Scott continues. 'We'd
located a place called Camp Blanding in northern Florida, a military compound that the Navy had pulled out of seven years ago. It's
being used by the National Guard now. Somehow we managed to
negotiate our way in there. Then we overhauled the place and used
it as our primary location for *Jane*'s SEAL Training Camp, Naval
Base and obstacle course.'

The heart of *G.I. Jane*, of course, *is* its gruelling training
sequences. But as Scott notes, 'The SEAL training you see in the
film is a bit of the real and the fanciful, mixed together. For
instance, to research what SEAL trainees go through, first I
observed the real thing, and then I went to bases at Parris Island
and Pensacola [Florida] to watch basic training exercises. But in a
funny kind of way, those weren't very photogenic – they were more
repetitious than anything else.

'That's why I decided to mix fact with invention. For instance,
the stuff with the recruits hauling their rubber rafts in and out of

the sea? That was real. So were the scenes where the trainees had
to stand for hours holding the same rafts over their heads. But a lot
of the stuff on the live fire obstacle course where Demi and the
guys are having real explosives chucked at them, for instance, was
exaggerated.'

In addition to the film's staged training exercises, Scott and
Military Technical Advisor Harry Humphries also subjected the
principal *G.I. Jane* actors to an aggressive two-week pre-production 'boot camp'. During this period the actors were subjected to
the same psychological harassment used by SEAL instructors on
real trainees, and taught many of the identical skills learned during the actual 17-week-long SEAL training course. Demi Moore
participated in all of this – the actor also performed many of her
own stunts in *G.I. Jane* (including an iconic scene of a T-shirted
O'Neil doing one-handed push-ups). In fact, such was Moore's
physical stamina and complete commitment to the role that she
was sometimes mistaken for her own stunt double.

As for the scene showing O'Neil shaving her head down to the
scalp (in order to adopt the same hairstyle worn by the male SEAL
recruits), this was also really done by Moore. Her dedication did
not go unappreciated; a small group of men who had visited the set
that day, specifically to see if the actor would actually shave her
head, reportedly cheered Moore's courage once her long, dark
tresses hit the stage floor.

Like *Thelma and Louise*, *1492* and *White Squall* before it, most
of *G.I. Jane* was shot on location (underlining Scott's affinity for
documentary-like realism). Many of the film's Washington, DC
sequences were shot in and around the Capitol; however, the 'Iraqi
desert' on which O'Neil is blooded at the film's end (after her unit
is sent to the Middle East on a rescue operation) was really filmed
on the parched landscapes of Lone Pine, California.

Unfortunately, *G.I. Jane*'s climax is both unnecessary and anticlimactic. Viewers have already seen Lt O'Neil win the respect and
admiration of her male colleagues by the middle of the third act;
sending her out to the Middle East simply to show off Jordan's
newly acquired fighting skills (and so that she can rescue Urgayle,
her principal tormentor) seems not only redundant, but seriously
robs the film of the cumulative dramatic power it has already
earned.

With Demi Moore during the shooting of G.I. Jane. **Moore demonstrated remarkable dedication to her role of Lt Jordan O'Neil, going so far as to shave off her long hair for the part. She also built herself up physically and was so convincing on set that she was often mistaken for her stunt double.**

Other problems haunted the film after its release. The American-Arab Anti-Discrimination Committee, for example, accused its distributor (the Walt Disney company) of racial discrimination during 'a gratuitous end sequence with star Demi Moore and her Navy SEAL chums on a rampage killing Arabs'. A more widespread criticism attacked a sequence showing O'Neil's unit being captured and interrogated by SEAL instructors posing as the enemy. During this training exercise, Master Chief Urgayle brutally beats and tortures O'Neil, who refuses to break under his abuse. Instead, the woman defiantly tells Urgayle to 'Suck my dick!' – a statement that, given its context, is both bizarrely comic and surreally appropriate.

Yet this intense sequence – which reportedly caused certain female audience members at a *G.I. Jane* pre-release screening in London to wince and cover their eyes – was, according to Scott, simply an unpleasant reflection of reality.

'Real SEALs have been ordered by the Navy to stay silent for 12 hours after they're captured by an enemy, even if they're being tortured during that period. That's so that any information they've been carrying before they were captured can be quickly changed if an enemy gets them. During my researches, I'd also come across two different cases of men who'd had to drop out of the SEAL programme because they couldn't take the same kind of POW interrogation training I showed Demi going through. And a real SEAL commander probably would select someone he perceived to be the weakest trainee during such an exercise, then try to break that person. So I thought it was only realistic to show Urgayle interrogating O'Neil in that way.'

G.I. Jane went into general release (in the United States) on 22 August 1997. The film's first weekend was very profitable, and by late December Scott's tenth feature had grossed $80 million worldwide. Still, while these numbers are significant, *G.I. Jane* was not the unqualified hit that it initially seemed poised to be. This is somewhat puzzling, since *Jane* is definitely the most mainstream and viewer-friendly of Scott's recent features. The film moves quickly, has a near-perfect focus on the engaging characters of Master Chief Urgayle and Lt O'Neil, and efficiently reworks Hollywood's well-established formula of the beleaguered individual successfully challenging an oppressive group.

'Many people misread this picture,' says Scott. 'It is pro-women, not anti. I was trying to show [once again] what a woman hs to do just to have the same chances [as men], and here's a woman fighting back and refusing to be beaten down.'

On the other hand, *Jane* is also among the most depersonalized of Scott's recent works. Even after acknowledging its serious subtext, or granting its inclusion of such interesting technical innovations as the 'jittery zoom' that Scott invented to punch up the film's climactic battle scene, *G.I. Jane* ultimately seems somewhat remote. Also, the manner in which its prominent woman's issue is presented is unnecessarily simplistic and cynical.

However, Scott was satisfied with the film. 'I think we got a fairly good sense of really being inside the military, and of how hidden agendas motivate politics,' the director says. 'As for its so-called feminist angle, I thought *G.I. Jane* just reflected the way the world is really working. I mean, a week before we started principal photography, American news services were running stories on how a young woman was trying to get into the Citadel, this all-male military school in South Carolina. So in general, I was quite pleased with the picture. My main disappointment was that I thought it would do better.'

If nothing else, *Jane* once again confirmed Scott's reputation as a director whose technical skills knew no limits. Yet in the arena of serious cinema, such mastery of technique means very little, especially in and of itself. The greater question then becomes – is Ridley Scott also a director who still has something to say?

I would hope, dear reader, that by now this book has supplied enough evidence to let your own answer to that question be a firm, unqualified 'Yes'.

10 New Horizons

Despite appearances, the final chapter in the book of Ridley Scott has yet to be written. For Scott is still going strong today – still directing, still producing, still developing new companies and exploring new interests.

Example: the Scotts and their associates recently purchased part of The Mill, a respected British digital effects house, which Ridley plans to incorporate as an on-site F/X facility for Shepperton Studios, as well as creating Mill Film for the international film industry.

Example: RSA still create some of the world's most stunning television and film commercials.

Example: Scott Free continues to develop new motion pictures and television films. Among these are the recent black comedy *Clay Pigeons* (1998), the shot-in-Canada *Where the Money Is* (with Paul Newman, Linda Fiorentino and Dermot Mulroney), and *RKO 281*, a $10 million, made-for-HBO TV film directed by Ben (*The Young Poisoner's Handbook*) Ross, which concerns Orson Welles' behind-the-scenes struggles to film *Citizen Kane*.

Ridley Scott's own directorial career also continues apace. Throughout much of 1998, the British film-maker worked on a big-budget adaptation (for Warner Brothers) of author Richard Matheson's influential contemporary vampire novel, *I Am Legend* (1954). Matheson's still-gripping book – regarding the last normal man's struggle to exist on an Earth devastated by biological warfare, one that has mutated every other survivor into human vampires – has already been filmed twice before (and badly) as *The Last Man on Earth* (1964), with Vincent Price, and *The Omega*

Man (1971), starring Charlton Heston. Scott's version was slated to feature action star Arnold Schwarzengger. But some months into the process, Warners pulled the plug on *I Am Legend* after attempts to bring the film's budget under $100 million failed.

Budgetary considerations were not the only reason, however; Scott also declined to pursue the film because he felt he had not been given enough time to revise *Legend*'s screenplay (which he found dramatically wanting). 'God knows I didn't want *I Am Legend* to be a "fang movie",' says the director. 'I did want the vampires to look monstrous, but we had difficulty with making them look monstrous without humanizing them. Then they started to become too human-looking, which became a huge problem. So we let that one go.'

Luckily, one of the best screenplays to cross Scott's desk in recent years was also presented to the director in 1998, not long after *I Am Legend* folded. This was David Franzoni's *Gladiator* (rewritten by John Logan), which began principal photography in February 1999. *Gladiator*'s narrative is set against the provinces and cities of the ancient Roman Empire; its protagonist is General Maximus, to be played by the Australian actor Russell Crowe, star of *LA Confidential* and *Romper Stomper*. Maximus falls victim to a cunning plot devised by the newly appointed Emperor of Rome, Commodus (*U-Turn* and *8mm*'s Joaquin Phoenix), and is stripped of both his lofty military position and Roman citizenship. The former general is then forced to fight repeatedly for his life as a gladiator in the Roman arenas.

A $100 million joint Universal/Dreamworks production which Scott will shoot in England, Malta and Morocco, '*Gladiator* excites me because it unfolds in a world completely different from ones I'd previously explored,' he explains. 'I hope to design the film in such a way that when people see it, they'll think, "Gee, Rome's never been done like *this* before." Because I've decided to do ancient Rome like Bombay; you'll see architecture that's only supposed to be a year old in the story, and right alongside it will be architecture that's 800 years old. Benjamin Fernandez, who did some art direction on *Alien* for me, is taking an actual section of a Moroccan Casbah and grafting a small provincial Roman arena on to it. We're building a full-scale Coliseum, too, in Malta. There's an old Napoleonic parade ground there which is already surrounded by pre-existing Romanesque limestone architecture, so that gives us like a two million dollar start on the set budget. And of course the arena games themselves will be pretty exotic.' (Sadly, *Gladiator* co-star Oliver Reed, originally picked to play 'Proximo', died of a heart attack during production – in a Maltese pub – on 2 May 1999.)

Although it is of course too early to assess *Gladiator* (since it is not yet completed), the film's screenplay reads like a promising admixture of *Spartacus* and *The Fall of the Roman Empire*. One can only hope that Franzoni and Logan's entertaining script will spark the monster hit that has so far has eluded Scott during the 1990s. If nothing else, one certainly looks forward to seeing just how this director, with his prodigious knowledge of art history and impressive talent for deeply layered production design, will portray the ancient Roman Empire!

By early 1999, Ridley Scott also had much to be grateful for on the personal front. Although his father Francis Percy Scott died in 1978, by 1999 Ridley's mother has already celebrated her ninety-third birthday, and all of his three children are now following in Scott's professional footsteps. Son Luke and daughter Jordan write and direct music videos, while eldest son Jake Scott has recently directed his first feature film, *Plunkett and Macleane*. All three children are also commercials directors and Ridley Scott's voice swells with fatherly pride when he speaks of their achievements.

Yet when all is said and done, Ridley Scott still remains something of an enigma. This is a man who emcompasses both the perceptive soul of an artist and the brain of a tough-minded businessman. Perhaps these sometimes opposing characteristics are one more reason why – to return to a observation first put forth in the introduction to this book – the full worth of Scott's cinema still has not been given its proper due.

In any event, *Ridley Scott: The Making of His Movies* is now rapidly coming to its close. And there remain only two last questions to ask.

With over two decades of directorial experience behind him, what does Scott see as a film's director's most important function?

Well [Scott replies], the more I produce, the more I realize that the most important person on a movie, once you've started the process, is the director.

Because without that concept you've got no order. To use an orchestral analogy, the director is the conductor, and a conductor is there to get the best out of each section of the orchestra, ranging from the timpani to the strings to the brass. He must orchestrate all that, put the different instruments together so that the music comes out sounding great. That's one vital function.

Another important part of a director's job is to extract the best out of everybody. The smoothest way to do that is with authority, which I think comes with time. Once you have it, people will usually listen to you with respect, and the general film-making process then isn't as stressful. In fact, I think most of the units who've worked on my films would say that it's been damn hard work, sure, but that we also usually have pretty good fun. Because it has to be fun. It has to be interesting for everybody. I still say that the actual making of a movie is gloriously inspirational, in fact, and stimulating, although it is also naturally stressful. But in a very good way, since it's the kind of stress that keeps you alive, as opposed to the stress that slowly kills you. Therefore, another part of directing is making sure that even the guy doing the smallest job is enthused, so that I get the best out of him.

Now comes the final question, one that has amused the film-maker throughout his career: how does Ridley Scott respond to the accusation that he is a director of 'more style than substance'?

With his typical straightforwardness, mainstream cinema's most vaunted visual stylist immediately replies to that query – in a manner that may surprise those expecting a tie-in to his highly-publicized imagistic obsessions.

What you put on the screen has to be fundamentally important, even if only for the moment. It has to say something that moves the audience; it must entertain, enchant and, perhaps above all, involve them. So the most important element of my films is always the screenplay. I must be able to hang my hopes and fears on what's inside the writer's head.

Yet the toughest part is also always the screenplay, every time. Movie-making is really all story, story, story [concludes Ridley Scott]. Everything else follows that.

Variety

THE

REVIEWS

THE DUELLISTS

Wednesday, June 1, 1977

Cannes, May 31. (BRITISH/COLOR)
CIC release of Enigma production. Stars Keith Carradine, Harvey Keitel. Directed by Ridley Scott. Screenplay, Gerald Vaughan-Hughes from the story by Joseph Conrad; camera (color), Frank Tidy; editor, Pamela Power; art director, Bryan Graves. Reviewed at Cannes Film Festival (competing), May 23, '77. Running time, 95 MINS.

D'Hubert	Keith Carradine
Feraud	Harvey Keitel
Adele	Cristina Raines
Colonel	Edward Fox
Treillard	Robert Stephens
Commander	John McEnery
Fouche	Albert Finney
Laura	Diana Quick

The film is a series of duels by two Napoleonic lieutenants during the early years of the 19th century. It delves into military codes of honor and its counterpart of violence for its own sake. But what the film sells is a series of carefully posed tableaus of period action and repose in colorful military days and rarely transcends this for a more robust portrayal of military life.

The Napoleonic Wars are behind this stubborn sword slashing and then pistols of two men whose personalities are caught up in their own personal vendetta within the epic European battles of the times. Harvey Keitel is an almost obsessed dueller who is asked to appear before the general due to his duels by Keith Carradine who practically volunteers for the job.

However, Keitel takes umbrage despite Carradine's act of duty and a first duel occurs with Carradine having the upper hand only to be jumped by a woman friend of Keitel's to stop it. Then follows another and they get increasingly savage with one taking place in ruins as they hack themselves into exhaustion with sabres.

The film poses the use of this constant battling by other soldiers for excitement and keeping up military myths and differing higher officer and political outlooks. Film goes on through the campaigns as the men slash their way even on horseback one time. Finally Carradine spares Keitel and insists that he, Keitel, is now dead for him and to go away.

Director Ridley Scott, reportedly from ad pix, does have an eye for fine compositions, period recreation and arresting tableaus. But it is somewhat surface and too taken up with poses, a feeling for candlelit interiors and a general statement on obsession and military codes if it rarely illuminates the deeper human aspects of these two flailing men.

Keitel is jaunty and menacing and Carradine more determined and a bit troubled but also caught up in this strange need of one to prove honor and the other slaking a twisted nature. It does not quite achieve a more lusty visual feel for the times and the strange relations of these two men to themselves and to the women in and out of their lives.

Director Scott bows with a definite flair for bright surfaces though he needs more care in blending it with a more cohesive and revealing background to remove a sort of glossy treatment. Fine thesps in smaller roles help with even Albert Finney in as the Napoleonic head of the Paris police. It should have a fine European career with U.S. chances calling for careful sell for best results for this arty swashbuckler.

–Mosk.

ALIEN

Wednesday, May 23, 1979

Another hot summer at the Fox-office. Hollywood, May 17. (COLOR)

A 20th Century-Fox release of a Brandywine-Ronald Shusett Production, produced by Gordon Carroll, David Giler and Walter Hill. Directed by Ridley Scott. Exec producer, Ronald Shusett. Screenplay, Dan O'Bannon. Camera (Eastman Color), Derek Vanlint; editor, Terry Rawlings; sound (Dolby), Derrick Leather; production design, Michael Seymour; art direction, Les Dilley, Roger Christian; special effects, Brian Johnson, Nick Allder; costumes, John Mollo; assistant director, Paul Ibbetson; music, Jerry Goldsmith. Reviewed at Samuel Goldwyn Theatre, Beverly Hills, Calif., May 16, 1979. (MPAA Rating: R.) Running time: 124 MINS.

Dallas	Tom Skerritt
Ripley	Sigourney Weaver
Lambert	Veronica Cartwright
Brett	Harry Dean Stanton
Kane	John Hurt
Ash	Ian Holm
Parker	Yaphet Kott

Twentieth Century-Fox has another goodie for the summer. Or as they say in the world of science, when your Celsius is soaring, your Celsius is soaring.

Plainly put, "Alien" is an old-fashioned scary movie set in a highly realistic sci-fi future, made all the more believable by the expert technical craftmanship that the industry just gets better and better at. Picture isn't quite good enough to be a combination of "The Exorcist" and "Star Wars," but both titles are likely to come to mind as word-of-mouth spreads rapidly.

Dan O'Bannon's script has more loose ends than the Pittsburgh Steelers but that doesn't matter as director Ridley Scott, cameraman Derek Vanlint and composer Jerry Goldsmith propel the emotions relentlessly from one visual surprise – and horror – to the next.

The price paid for the excitement, and it's a small one, is very little involvement with the characters themselves. Often, in fact, it's hard to tell what they're doing or why. But it really doesn't matter when the screaming starts.

In contrast to the glamorous adventurous outer-space life often depicted in sci-fi, "Alien" initially presents a mundane commercial spacecraft with crew members like Yaphet Kotto bitching and moaning about wages and working conditions.

The tedium is shared by captain Tom Skerritt, his aide Sigourney Weaver and

the rest of the crew, Veronica Cartwright, Harry Dean Stanton, John Hurt and Ian Holm, a generally good cast in the concededly cardboard roles. Eventually, it will be Weaver who gets the biggest chance in her film debut and she carries it off well.

Since they were doomed to get an R rating for gore, anyway, the film-makers have thrown in some 20th century swearing for Weaver, which seems odd and awkward in the context, plus a bit of a skin show that's fetching but a little far-fetched.

–Har.

BLADE RUNNER

Wednesday, June 16, 1982

Brilliantly made, dramatically muddled look into the future. Will divide critics and public. Hollywood, June 12. (COLOR)

A Ladd Company release in association with Sir Run Run Shaw through Warner Bros. of a Michel Deeley-Ridley Scott production. Produced by Deeley. Directed by Scott. Executive producers, Brian Kelly, Hampton Fancher. Stars Harrison Ford. Screenplay, Fancher, David Peoples, based on the novel "Do Androids Dream of Electric Sheep" by Philip K. Dick. Camera (Technicolor, Panavision), Jordan Cronenweth; supervising editing, Terry Rawlings; editor, Marsha Nakashima; music, Vangelis; production design, Lawrence G. Paull; art direction, David Snyder; set design, Tom Duffield, Bill Skinner, Greg Pickrell, Charles Breen, Louis Mann, David Klasson; set decoration, Linda DeScenna, Tom Roysden, Leslie Frankenheimer; special photo-graphic effects supervisors, Douglas Trumbull, Richard Yuricich, David Dryer; visual futurist, Syd Mead; costume design, Charles Knode, Michael Kaplan; sound (Dolby), Bud Alper; associate producer, Ivor Powell; assistant directors, Newton Arnold, Peter Cornberg. Reviewed at The Burbank Studios, Burbank, June 11, 1982. (MPAA Rating: R.) Running time: 114 MINS.

Deckard ....Harrison Ford
Batty..................................Rutger Hauer
Rachel ....Sean Young
Gaff.......................Edward James Olmos
Bryant..........................M. Emmet Walsh
Pris ....Daryl Hannah
Sebastian ....William Sanderson
Leon ....Brion James
Tyrell..Joe Turkel
Zhora ....Joanna Cassidy
Chew ....James Hong
Holden...............................Morgan Paull
Bear.............................Kevin Thompson
Kaiser......................John Edward Allen
Taffrey Lewis ....Hy Pyke

"Blade Runner" undoubtedly constitutes the most riveting – and depressing – vision of the near-future since "A Clockwork Orange." Ridley Scott's first picture since "Alien" is a stylistically dazzling film noir set 37 years hence in a brilliantly imagined Los Angeles marked by both technological wonders and horrendous squalor. Special effects and sheer virtuosity of the production will attract considerable attention, but unrelenting grimness and vacuum at the story's center will make it tough to recoup reported $30,000,000 budget, not to mention ad-promo costs. Critical reaction will probably vary widely.

Basic premise taken from a novel by the late Philip K. Dick provides a strong dramatic hook – replicants, robots designed to supply "Off World" slave labor, are outlawed on earth. But a few of them have infiltrated L.A., and retired enforcer Harrison Ford is recruited to eliminate them before they can do any damage.

Replicants appear totally human, are as smart as and sometimes stronger than their makers, and are deficient only in real memories and soul. One of them, beautiful Sean Young, is an advanced model with implanted memories so "real" that even she doesn't know she's a replicant until she's tested by Ford.

She's the ultimate wrong woman to fall for, and naturally, Ford does. Unfortunately, what could have been a strong emotional core of the film, as well as a good little parable for the importance of feelings, is scanted in the execution – Young disappears for long stretches at a time, and at others Ford merely sits morosely around his apartment staring at photographs, which slows up the action.

Ford's frequent inertia also mutes the detective angle of the story, which is couched in some hard-boiled, Chandleresque narration and in the long run proves to be the weakest aspect of the pic. Scott and his collaborators have devoted considerable thought to virtually every other aspect of their undertaking, but haven't sufficiently adjusted or freshened up the basic narrative framework of the old-fashioned plot to make it jibe with their main interests.

Film begins with a stunning aerial introduction to futuristic L.A., a cesspool dominated by brightly lit steel-and-glass towers, neon signs and smoothly flying vehicles. Down on the ground, however, a polyglot population wanders the anarchic streets, which intersect to create an impression of Cairo, Tokyo, Times Square and L.A. all rolled into one.

Scott's L.A. is clearly capitalistic, but no political power structure is mentioned, just as possible climate changes are ignored as a reason why it always seems to be raining. Costumes and hairstyles possess a vaguely punk look, and introduction of the replicants into this threatening, nightmarish environment creates a superb amplification of urban paranoia where one can never know who to trust, so you don't trust anybody.

Dramatically, film is virtually taken over at the midway point by top replicant Rutger Hauer. After destroying his creator in a murder of Shakespearean dimensions, the massive, albino-looking Hauer takes off after Ford, and the villain here is so intriguing and charismatic that, in Hitchcock fashion, one almost comes to prefer him to the most stolid, methodical hero. Ultimate confrontation between the two on a rooftop is highly effective, although the coda involving Ford and Young (who's virtually been forgotten at this point) seems almost like an afterthought (ending was reportedly tinkered with in sneak previews).

A few real locations, such as the Bradbury Building, have been used, but essentially "Blade Runner" is an ultimate studio picture. Production designer Lawrence G. Paull, art director David Snyder and the sizeable contingent of set designers and set decorators have created an extraordinary visual spectacle, just as special photographic effects supervisors Douglas Trumbull, Richard Yuricich and David Dryer have worked overtime to contribute to the futuristic verisimilitude.

Lenser Jordan Cronenweth and composer Vangelis have also done superior work here. On every level, the technical brilliance of the achievement is continually compelling. Dramatically, film isn't all it should have been, but this is nevertheless a major entry in the futuristic genre.

Pic was finanaced by various sources, and Jerry Perenchio and Bud Yorkin receive credit as presentors.

–Cart.

LEGEND

Wednesday, August 21, 1985

Lavishly produced but thin-scripted fantasy. London, Aug. 19. (U.S.-COLOR) **A 20th Century Fox (Universal Pictures in U.S.) release of a Legend Production. Produced by Arnon Milchan. Directed by Ridley Scott. Features entire cast. Screenplay, William Hjortsberg; camera (Panavision, Fujicolor), Alex Thomson; editor, Terry Rawlings; music, Jerry Goldsmith; special makeup, Rob Bottin; production design, Assheton Gorton; costumes, Charles Knode; special effects supervisor, Nick Allder; production supervisor, Hugh Harlow; choreography, Arlene Phillips; 1st assistant directors, Garth Thomas, Bill Westley; additional photography, Max Mowdray, Harry Oakes; supervising art directors, Norman Dorme, Les Dilley; set decorator, Ann Mollo; coproducer, Tim Hampton; The Rob Bottin Crew: Production manager, Richard White; sculptural design, Henry Alvarez; lead special make-up artist, Vince Prentice; lab technician supervisor, John Goodwin; cosmetic print supervisor, Margaret Beserra; Visual Optical Effects: Matte photography consultant, Stanley Sayer, Fotherly Ltd., Peerless Camera Co. Reviewed at National Film Theater, London, Aug. 18, 1985. Running time: 94 MINS.**

Jack	Tom Cruise
Princess Lili	Mia Sara
Darkness	Tim Curry
Gump	David Bennent
Blix	Alice Playten
Screwball	Billy Barty
Brown Tom	Cork Hubbert

"Legend" contains all the exhilarating visual elements audiences have come to expect from Ridley Scott. It is a fairy-tale produced on a grand scale, a classic tale of the struggle between darkness and light, good and evil, set in some timeless world and peopled with fairies, elves and goblins, plus a spectacularly satisfying Satan.

At the same time, the basic premise is alarmingly thin, a compendium of any number of ancient fairytales including "Jack and The Beanstalk" and "The Sleeping Beauty," with borrowings from dramatic works such as "A Midsummer Night's Dream" and "Peter Pan." Plot concerns a heroic young peasant, Jack, who takes his sweetheart, Princess Lili, to see the most poweful creatures on earth, the last surviving unicorns. Unknown to the young lovers, Darkness, (i.e., The Devil) is using the innocence of Lili as a bait to trap and emasculate the unicorns, and succeeds in removing the horn of the male beast, triggering an instant ice-age. Soon after, Darkness kidnaps the princess, intending to have her as his bride. It's up to intrepid Jack, and a friendly band of elves, to come to the rescue.

Perhaps realizing that the plot mechanics aren't very interesting, Scott has kept them to a minimum and concentrated on the action and the bizarre, magical characters. All too often, though, Williams Hjortsberg's script contains such deliberately anachronistic lines as "Time goes fast when you're having fun" or "I get the point, Lord," which may be intended humorously, but which fall pretty flat. Another minus is the rather insipid hero, as played by Tom Cruise.

Kids of all ages should be entranced by the magnificent make-up effects of Rob Bottin and his crew, from the smallest elves to the giant Darkness. The latter is unquestionably the most impressive depiction of Satan ever brought to the screen. Tim Curry plays him majestically with huge horns, cloved feet, red, leathery flesh and yellow eyes, plus a resonantly booming voice. Pic's best scene comes when he threatens the lovely Lili and she tells him he's an animal: "We're all animals, my dear," he replies.

Also registering strongly is David Bennent (the lead in "The Tin Drum" a few years back) as a knowing pixie with large, pointed ears. Annabelle Lanyon is also very effective as a jealous fairy, apparently based on J. M. Barrie's Tinkerbell. As clumsy elves, Bill Barty and Cork Hubbert provide plenty of fun.

Ironically, for a film that celebrates nature, "Legend" was almost entirely lensed on the large Bond set at Pinewood (production was interrupted by a fire which destroyed the set). It is technically wondrous to behold, but the very slender basis on which so much imagination and expertise is resting makes it a rather fragile production. Terry Rawlings'

editing has resulted in a very tight 94-minute running time, leaving audiences no time to ponder the script's inadequacies. Jerry Goldsmith's score is one of his best.

"Legend" is set to open the Venice Film Fest Aug. 26, but theatrical openings have been put back until year's end. With it legendary elements, it does seem more of a Christmas film than a summer one, but it will have to be handled carefully if results commensurate with the big budget are to be achieved.

–Strat

Mike Keegan	Tom Berenger
Claire Gregory	Mimi Rogers
Ellie Keegan	Lorraine Bracco
Lt. Garber	Jerry Orbach
Neil Steinhart	John Rubinstein
Joey Venza	Andreas Katsulas
T.J.	Tony DiBenedetto
Koontz	James Moriarty
Win Hockings	Mark Moses
Scotty	Daniel Hugh Kelly
Tommy	Harley Cross

SOMEONE TO WATCH OVER ME

Wednesday, September 30, 1987

Stylish thriller overcomes script implausibilities. (COLOR)

A Colombia Pictures release of a Thierry de Ganay production. Produced by De Ganay, Harold Schneider. Executive producer and directed by Ridley Scott. Screenplay, Howard Franklin; camera (Deluxe color), Steven Poster; editor, Claire Simpson; music, Michael Kamen; sound (Dolby), Gene Cantamessa; production design, Jim Bissell; set decoration, Linda de Scenna; assistant director, Joseph P. Reidy; production manager, Max Stein, N. Y. – Bill Gerrity; costume design, Colleen Atwood; stunt coordinators, Glenn Wilder, Ronnie Rondell; associate producer, Mimi Polk; casting, Joy Todd. Reviewed at Columbia 5th Avenue screening room, N. Y., Sept. 23, 1987. (MPAA Rating: R.) Running time: 106 MINS.

"Someone To Watch Over Me" is a stylish and romantic police thriller which manages, through the sleek direction of Ridley Scott and persuasive ensemble performances, to triumph over several hard-to-swallow plot developments. Benefitting from topliner Tom Berenger's post-"Platoon" prominence, pic stands to do well at the fall box-office in a year totally dominated by police and crime films.

Berenger portrays Mike Keegan, a happily married N. Y. cop from the Bronx who has just been promoted to detective and finds himself assigned on the night shift to protect socialite Claire Gregory (Mimi Rogers), witness to a brutal murder. The heinous killer, Joey Venza, played with economical nuance and menace by Andreas Katsulas, tracks

Gregory down at the Guggenheim Museum and terrorizes her in the ladies' room while Keegan is distracted. Though he subsequently chases Venza down and effects the collar, failure to read the goon his rights results in Venza back on the street and Gregory marked for death.

Though wife Lorraine Bracco and son Harley Cross are loveable and supportive, plot dictates that Berenger fall in love and bed down with the at first chilly Rogers. As with the current hit "Fatal Attraction," this infidelity is a key story element but a hurdle for the audience to believe. Even more difficult to swallow is a highly contrived climax: after his wife finds out about the affair and Berenger moves out, the killer kidnaps his wife and child, leading Berenger to bring Rogers to the scene in a hostage exchange ruse. Though suspenseful and well-staged, the violation of police procedure is incredible and unconvincing.

Papering over these holes in Howard Franklin's screenplay, director Scott consistently commands attention with his trademark visual style, which frequently turns the otherwise gritty, New York thriller into something out of his sci-fi epic "Blade Runner" (opening aerial shot of Manhattan, '40s music, smoked sets and backlit, fogged street scenes often evoke the prior film). Tech credits are all topnotch, though overuse of the title standard. whether warbled by Sting, Roberta Flack or played as an instrumental, proves counterproductive.

Berenger carries the film handily, utterly convincing as the working class stiff out of his element accompanying Rogers through her elegant apartment or posh parties. Rogers is alluring as the romantic interest, recalling the sharpness

and beauty of Laraine Day, while wife Bracco is fully sympathetic and easily has the viewer siding against the two leads during their hanky-panky segments. James Moriarty provides welcome comic relief as an uppity fellow cop while John Rubinstein is saddled with the thankless role of Rogers' creepy, rich boy friend.

—Lor.

BLACK RAIN

September 20–26, 1989

Hollywood

A Paramount Picture release of a Jaffe/Lansing production in association with Michael Douglas. Produced by Stanley R. Jaffe, Sherry Lansing. Executive producers, Craig Bolotin, Julie Kirkham. Directed by Ridley Scott. Screenplay, Bolotin, Warren Lewis; camera (Super 35, Technicolor), Jan DeBont; editor, Tom Rolf; music, Hans Zimmer; sound (Dolby), Keith A. Wester, James J. Sabat; production design, Norris Spencer; art direction, John J. Moore. Herman F. Zimmerman, Kazuo Takenaka (Japan); set design, Alan S. Kaye, Robert Maddy, James R. Bayliss; set decoration, John Alan Hicks, Leslie Bloom, Richard C. Goddard, John M. Dwyer, Kyoji Sasaki (Japan); costume design, Ellen Mirojnick; special effects supervisor, Stan Parks; second unit director, Bobby Bass; additional photography, Howard Atherton; aerial photography, David Nowell; additional editing, William Gordean, Jacqueline Cambas; line producer (Japan), Yosuke Mizuno; associate producer, Alan Poul; assistant directors, Aldric La'auli Porter, Benjamin

Rosenberg, Masayuki Taniguchi (Japan), Dennis Maguire (second unit); casting, Dianne Crittenden, Nobuaki Murooka (Japan); additional casting, Melissa Skoff. Reviewed at Mann National Theater, Westwood, Calif., Sept. 12, 1989. MPAA Rating: R. Running time: 126 MIN.

Nick	Michael Douglas
Charlie	Andy Garcia
Masahiro	Ken Takakura
Joyce	Kate Capshaw
Sato	Yusaku Matsuda
Ohashi	Shigeru Koyama
Oliver	John Spencer
Katayama	Guts Ishimatsu
Nashida	Yuya Uchida
Sugai	Tomisaburo Wakayama
Miyuki	Miyuki Ono

Since this is a Ridley Scott film, "Black Rain" is about 90% atmosphere and 10% story. But what atmosphere! This gripping crime thriller about the hardboiled N. Y. cop Michael Douglas tracking a yakuza hood in Osaka, Japan, boasts magnificent lensing by Jan DeBont and powerfully baroque production design by Norris Spencer. Though it may be too dark for some viewers, and cops out a bit in the overlong finale, the Paramount release looks like a b. o. winner.

Smoothly and intelligently blending the conventions of American film noir with those of Japanese yakuza (gangster) films, "Black Rain" is much more effective than its forerunner, Sydney Pollack's 1975 "The Yakuza," which also had Japanese icon Ken Takakura in a sidekick role to the American protagonist.

Until a misguided last-minute attempt to show that he's really a nice guy underneath, Douglas is utterly believable as a reckless and scummy homicide detective who takes kickbacks from drug dealers and resorts to the most brutal methods to capture escaped counterfeiter Yusaku Matsuda.

First collaring Matsuda after a shocking outbreak of violence in a N. Y. restaurant, Douglas is sent with him to Osaka, where he promptly loses him to the yakuza and watches helplessly as his partner Andy Garcia is murdered. Coming into conflict with the Japanese police, Douglas turns to the criminal underground to help bring in his prey.

Scripters Craig Bolotin (who also exec produced with Julie Kirkham) and Warren Lewis fascinatingly depict the growing influence of Takakura's higher concepts of honor and loyalty on Douglas, who in turn causes some of his expedient lack of morality to rub off on the Japanese police inspector.

It isn't long before the entire world begins to seem like "one big grey area," as the cynical Douglas describes New York City.

Lavishly backed up by producers Stanley R. Jaffe and Sherry Lansing – who overcame the hazards of a reportedly difficult location to help create a seamlessly exotic Osaka – Scott brings a "Black Runner"-like density to his smoggy, hellish visual stylization.

DeBont's Oscar-caliber lensing gives an electric intensity to a film which is never less than riveting to watch.

The mood of omnipresent menace and descent into an amoral quagmire is evocatively summed up in the film's title, a metaphor for the postwar corruption that spawned the yakuza. Crime boss Tomisaburo Wakayama, recalling the waves of American B-29s that firebombed Japanese cities in World War II, tells Douglas that Americans "made the black rain" and created an enduring climate for crime.

Though generally depicting the nearly psychotic Douglas character from a critical distance, Scott sometimes lapses into the too-frequent failings of contemporary pics and encourages the audience to cheer when Douglas gives the villain a gratuitous punch in the face or acts like Rambo in assaulting a gangster stronghold.

The clumsily sentimental ending seems to reflect an inability to come to terms with this complex s.o.b. of a cop. By attempting to sugarcoat him to let the audience to go out feeling good, "Black Rain" may succeed in doing just the opposite, squandering some of its earlier impressiveness.

Takakura's quiet sense of stature and Garcia's resigned acceptance of death are among the finest things in the film. The rest of the Japanese supporting cast is first-rate, particularly Wakayama's godfather. Although Kate Capshaw's film noir B-girl role is corny, she plays it with a suitably Claire Trevor-like heart of gold.

Tech credits are uniformly stunning.

—Mac.

THELMA & LOUISE

May 13, 1991

A Pathé Entertainment presentation of a Percy Main production. Produced by Ridley Scott, Mimi Polk. Directed by Scott. Screenplay, Callie Khouri; camera (color), Adrian Biddle; editor, Thom Noble; music, Hans Zimmer; sound, Keith A. Wester; production design, Norris Spencer; costume design, Elizabeth McBride; art direction, Lisa Dean; set decoration, Anne Ahrens; set design, Alan Kaye; assistant director, Steve Danton; 2nd unit director-stunt coordinator, Bobby Bass; coproducers, Dean O'Brien, Khouri. Reviewed at Pathé screening room, L.A., May 2, 1991. (In Cannes Film Festival, noncompeting.) MPAA rating: R. Running time: 128 MIN.

Lousie	Susan Sarandon
Thelma	Geena Davis
Hal	Harvey Keitel
Jimmy	Michael Madsen
Darryl	Christopher McDonald
J.D.	Brad Pitt

"Thelma & Louise" is a thumpingly adventurous road pic about two regular gals who shoot down a would-be rapist and wind up on the lam in their '66 T-bird. Even those who don't rally to pic's fed-up feminist

outcry will take to its comedy, momentum and dazzling visuals. This could be the pic that drags sidelined MGM/Pathé back out onto the road.

"I'd rather be a killer than a victim," decides reluctant cop Harrison Ford near the outset of Ridley Scott's "Blade Runner," and the director uses the same theme to kick off the saga of Arkansas housewife Thelma (Geena Davis) and waitress Louise (Susan Sarandon).

Setting out for a weekend fishing trip away from the drudgery of their lives and the indifference of their men, they stop at a roadside honkytonk to blow off steam, and things turn ugly. A guy tries to rape Thelma; Louise can't take it so she plugs the creep wtih a .38. Then they hit the highway, dazed and in trouble.

It's a tricky scene: She didn't have to kill him, but it's a welcome move. Shookup Thelma wants to know why they don't just tell the police what happened. "Who's gonna believe you," retorts Louise. "We don't live in that kind of world."

Sarandon is the big sister; more feminine, more focused, smoldering with a quiet determination. The car's hers and she drives it. Davis is more loosely wrapped; she goes with the flow, follows her whims into trouble, but also discovers untapped capacities in herself. They're not man-haters; they can't seem to stay away from men.

They're just out for freedom and a good time, and though the trip quickly turns miserable and all seems ruined, the more trouble they get into, oddly enough, the more fun they have. The journey into recklessness is exhilarating, which gives the film its buoyant pull.

Scott, working from an original script by Callie Khouri, is also having fun – too

much, now and then, in certain over-the-top scenes. But the helmer seems to be telling the audience this is just a movie. Don't expect to believe it, just get ready for the big finish.

It's big all right, and in an indelible final image, it maintains the sense of reckless exhilaration to the end, thus qualifying as a triumph.

This is a journey film where the characters find a whole lot more than they knew they were looking for when they started out. "I think I've found my calling," says Thelma at one point. "Something's crossed over in me. I can't go back."

Despite some delectably funny scenes between the sexes, Scott's latest pic isn't about women vs. men. It's about freedom, like any good road picture. In that sense, and in many others, it's a classic.

Visuals and music ride shotgun with the story here, and Scott, a Brit, has conjured more magic from the American Southwest landscape than any drug-free individual is likely to see.

California and southern Utah locales stand in for Arkansas, Oklahoma and Texas, but via Scott's vision and the superb Panavision lensing of cinematographer Adrian Biddle ("Alien"), the sites take on a mythic luster.

The screen yields them remarkable depth, space and clarity, and Scott fills it with savory images: A young cowboy (Brad Pitt) is seen through the T-bird's drop-spattered plastic rear window dancing in the rain.

Just as important is the music, whether it's country & western-tinged warbling from jukeboxes and bandstands or Hans Zimmer's twanging, shimmering score.

Sarandon and Davis have found a dream vehicle here, and they drive it.

Davis, who starts out a ditz, blossoms into a stylish, take-charge criminal. "You be sweet to your wife," she tells a blubbering cop as she helps him into the trunk of his car. "My husband wasn't sweet to me, and look how I turned out."

Michael Madsen, a standout in a small part in "The Doors," puts in another strong bid for attention as Sarandon's bull-headed b.f. Pitt is sharp and beguiling as the young outlaw hitchhiker, and Harvey Keitel successfully sheds his Eastern edges for a soft Southern drawl and a sympathetic manner.

Delayed from an originally planned March opening by MGM/Pathé's merger-related financial troubles, pic is now set for nationwide release May 24. It screens out of competition at Cannes on closing night.

—*Daws.*

1492: CONQUEST OF PARADISE

October 12, 1992

(British–French–Spanish)

A Paramount release of a Percy Main / Legende / Cyrk production. Produced by Ridley Scott, Alain Goldman. Executive producers, Mimi Polk Sotela, Iain Smith. Co-producers, Marc Boyman, Roselyne Bosch, Pere Fages. Directed by Scott. Screenplay, Bosch. Camera (Rank color; Panavision widescreen), Adrian Biddle; editors, William Anderson, Françoise Bonnot; music, Vangelis; production design, Norman Spencer; supervising art directors, Benjamin Fernandez, Leslie Tomkins; art direction, Raul Antonio Paton, Kevin Phipps, Martin Hitchcock, Luke Scott; set decoration, Ann Mollo; costume design, Charles Knode, Barbara Rutter; sound (Dolby), Pierre Gamet; associate producer, Garth Thomas; assistant director, Terry Needham; special effects supervisor, Kit West; 2nd unit director, Hugh Johnson; casting, Louis Digiaimo. Reviewed at Village Theater, L.A., Oct. 1, 1992. MPAA Rating: PG13. Running time: 150 MIN.

Columbus	Gérard Depardieu
Sanchez	Armand Assante
Queen Isabel	Sigourney Weaver
Older Fernando	Loren Dean
Beatrix	Angela Molina
Marchena	Fernando Rey
Noxica	Michael Wincott
Pinzon	Tcheky Karyo
Capt. Mendez	Kevin Dunn
Santangel	Frank Langella
Bobadilla	Mark Margolis
Arojaz	Kario Salem
Fernando (age 10)	Billy Sullivan
Brother Buyl	John Heffernan
Guevara	Arnold Vosloo
Bartolome	Steven Waddington
Giacomo	Fernando G. Cuervo
Alonso	Jose Luis Ferrer
Utapan	Bercelio Moya

All of Ridley Scott's vaunted visuals can't transform "1492" from a lumbering, one-dimensional historical fresco into the complex, ambiguous character study that it strives to be. Ambitious independent production often struggles to hold interest during the lengthy running time and, while the physical aspects of carving out a European presence in the New World

are often vividly evoked, bombast and pretention are in greater evidence than real drama and psychological insight. Interest in Scott, Gérard Depardieu and seeing the "real" Columbus film may spark some initial box office, but pic looks to have a short commercial voyage.

In contrast to recent revisionist attacks on the explorer's character and leading role in launching the European subjugation of native Americans, French journalist and first-time screenwriter Roselyne Bosch offers up a humanistic pacifist driven by an enigmatic mix of motives to settle a new land. "They are not savages, and neither will we be," he announces to his crew.

At the outset, Columbus is presented as both a visionary and a man of logic, a man allied with monks but disgusted by the Inquisition, a rationalist in an age of religious superstition, an adventurer among timid conformists. Crucially, he is able to charm the Spanish queen into sending him into the unknown. After a remarkably uneventful voyage spurred by one little inspirational speech to his nervous crew, Columbus reaches his promised "earthly paradise" and establishes a relatively benign relationship with the natives.

After his triumphant return home, a new, 17-ship expedition is launched. Ultimately, Columbus administrates ineptly and tries ineffectually to promote a policy of peaceful coexistence. Minds dominated by military ambition, religious fervor and greed inevitably gain the upper hand and turn the lush tropical settlement into a living hell.

Bosch has imposed this basic dramatic arc upon a very unwieldy life story which actually encompassed four voyages over 10 years. Unfortunately, for all the visual impact Scott brings to the saga, his dazzling muralistic style has the effect of flattening things out to the point where they have all the dimensionality of a medieval painting.

Relationships in the movie barely exist. When Queen Isabel informs Columbus that he can embark on a third journey, but without his brothers, it's unclear that he's had brothers along with him before (a problem compounded by the fact that one is played by a Brit, the other by a Spaniard). And is Angela Molina the hero's wife or mistress?

Scott takes slightly greater interest in the political dynamics informing the yarn. The Crown's treasurer (Armand Assante) plays out an ambiguous relationship with Columbus throughout all of the latter's changing fortunes, while three of the hero's principal adversaries are cast so that the actors' nasty looks say it all about their villainy (e.g., Michael Wincott's saboteur).

Sigourney Weaver briefly suggests a sexual susceptibility to Columbus behind the queen's approval of his grand scheme. But no one is allowed the opportunity to develop a character.

As for Depardieu's Columbus, the great French actor does his best to get his mouth around the long speeches and harangues, and is comprehensible most of the time. His energy, passion and conviction are ideal for the role, but perhaps it remains beyond him at this point to act in English in depth.

In this Scott film, the visuals are expected to virtually do it all. As beautiful as some of the images are, helmer is mostly straining for effect here, injecting fog and smoke into the frame at every opportunity (even, implausibly, in open water under clear skies), and finally succumbs to total overkill in the gruesome, thunderous scenes of colonial calamity.

Still, there are striking moments that stick in the mind. Columbus' first glimpse of the New World comes, breathtakingly, as some fog breaks, revealing a verdant jungle looming close behind it.

Overall, dramatic pacing is ponderous and indulgent, accentuated by Vangelis' occasionally effective but mostly overbearing wall-to-wall score.

Adrian Biddle's lensing is marked by the contrast between gloomy interiors streaked with window and candle light, and blindingly sunny exteriors. Norman Spencer's wonderfully detailed production design abets the multitude of actual medieval locations in Spain, and creates a convincingly ratty initial colonial village (North American sections were shot in Costa Rica). Charles Knode and Barbara Rutter's costume contributions are first-rate, as are other behind-the-scenes efforts.

Three major pics, including the stodgy British 1949 Fredric March biopic and the recent Salkind flop, have proven Columbus' story difficult to dramatize or put over with the public (ironically, all have been undertaken by foreign, not U.S., producers). It should be a while until anyone tries again.

—Todd McCarthy

WHITE SQUALL

January 29–February 4, 1996

A Buena Vista Pictures release of a Hollywood Pictures presentation in association with Largo Entertainment in a Scott Free production. Produced by Mimi Polk Gitlin, Rocky Lang. Executive producer, Ridley Scott. Co-producer, Nigel Wooll, Todd Robinson.

Directed by Ridley Scott. Screenplay, Todd Robinson. Camera (Technicolor color), Hugh Johnson; editor, Gerry Hambling; music, Jeff Rona; production design, Peter J. Hampton, Leslie Tomkins; art direction, Joseph P. Lucky; set decoration, Rand Sagers; costume design, Judianna Makovsky; sound (Dolby), Ken Weston; associate producer, Terry Needham; assistant director, Needham; second-unit director, David Tringham; unit production manager, Wooll; special effects, Joss Williams; casting, Louis Di Giaimo. Reviewed at Disney Studios screening room, Burbank, Jan. 26, 1966. MPAA Rating: PG–13. Running time: 127 MIN.

Sheldon "Skipper"	Jeff Bridges
Dr. Alice Sheldon	Caroline Goodall
McCrea	John Savage
Chuck Gieg	Scott Wolf
Frank Beaumont	Jeremy Sisto
Gil Martin	Ryan Phillippe
Robert March	David Lascher
Dean Preston	Eric Michael Cole
Shay Jennings	Jason Marsden
Francis Beaumont	David Selby
Girard Pascal	Julio Mechoso
Sanders	Zeljko Ivanek
Tod Johnstone	Balthazar Getty
Tracy Lapchick	Ethan Embry

Call it "Floating Poets Society," or perhaps "Dead Sailors Society," but this coming-of-age story, circa 1960, has much the same feel as that earlier release, with a group of teenage boys undergoing a rite of passage – under the tutelage of a stern mentor – by sailing around the Caribbean for a year. Director Ridley Scott's lavish production isn't totally satisfying, coasting aimlessly at times before suddenly leaping to a more intense dramatic plane. Pic could nevertheless leave a decent box office wake if younger audiences can be lured to this fact-based high-seas adventure.

Much of that may have to do with the appeal of "Party of Five" star Scott Wolf, who provides the movie's centerpiece and narrator as Chuck Gieg, a high-school senior through whose eyes the audience sees the boat's stern Skipper (Jeff Bridges) and his other, sometimes troubled classmates aboard the Albatross.

To that extent, in fact, as much as anything else, "White Squall" may be remembered as Wolf's coming-out party, given his teen heart-throb status on the marginally rated Fox series and seeming potential as box office draw.

The movie's foremost problem has to do with its structure. Pic takes plenty of time introducing its attractive, young cast as they bond while sailing around the Caribbean, before abruptly erupting into the storm sequence that claims several lives.

That, in turn, is followed by a brief, anticlimactic courtroom tribunal – a sort of poor man's "The Caine Mutiny" that, true story or not, feels a bit forced and contrived.

Each of the young men is plagued by his own demons, including Frank (Jeremy Sisto), who struggles against a domineering father; Gil (Ryan Phillippe), whose fear of heights stems from an earlier tragedy; and Dean (Eric Michael Cole), whose bullying ways hide insecurity about his academic skills.

Their interaction and inauguration aboard the ship provide plenty of amusing and moving moments but also long languid stretches, making one yearn for the storm to arrive.

When it finally does, it's worth the wait – a staggering, if at times confusing, sequence in which the boat is sunk and various members of the crew are lost.

Yet Scott and writer Todd Robinson take such a long time getting there that they don't really have time to do justice to the aftermath of those events. One example: Those without an academic interest in sailing might appreciate a brief explanation of what exactly a "white squall" is and why no one seems to believe in them.

In the same vein, the filmmakers take a rather facile, anachronistic "Ophrah" esque approach toward the boys' feelings about their families and the Skipper's role as a "tough Love"-minded surrogate father.

Bridges is appropriately stern in the role, though what drives him is never really explored, even through his relationship with his wife (Caroline Goodall), the ship's doctor. Wolf proves the perfect Everykid, brimming with fresh-faced likeability, while the rest of the cast is solid, with Cole the most notable standout.

Scott remains a gifted visual stylist, and cinematographer Hugh Johnson beautifully captures the open seas as well as the ship's confined spaces. Indeed, early shots when the crew has its first experience with rough waters are gut-churning enough that some audience members may feel queasy.

Other tech credits are equally inpressive, with St. Vincent, St. Lucia and Grenada providing the principal locales.

–Brian Lowry

G.I. JANE

August 11–17, 1997

'G.I. Jane' gets SEAL of approval

A Buena Vista release of a Hollywood Pictures presentation in association with Scott Free and Largo Entertainment of a Roger Birnbaum / Scott Free / Moving Pictures production. Produced by Birnbaum, Demi Moore, Suzanne Todd. Executive producers, Danielle Alexandra, Julie Bergman Sender, Chris Zarpas. Co-producer, Nigel Wooll.

Directed by Ridley Scott. Screenplay, David Twohy, Danielle Alexandra; story by Alexandra. Camera (Technicolor, Panavision widescreen), Hugh Johnson; editor, Pietro Scalia; music, Trevor Jones; production design, Arthur Max; supervising art director, Bill Hiney; art direction, Richard Johnson; set design, Thomas Minton; set decoration, Cindy Carr; costume design, Marilyn Vance; sound (Dolby), Keith A. Wester; stunt coordinator, Phil Neilson; associate producers, Terry Needham, Diane Minter Lewis, Tim McBride; assistant director, Needham; casting, Louis Di Giaimo, Brett Goldstein. Reviewed at the AMC Century City, L.A., July 24, 1997. MPAA Rating: R. Running time: 124 MIN.

Lt. Jordan O'Neil	Demi Moore
Master Chief	
John Urgayle	Viggo Mortensen
Sen. Lillian DeHaven	Anne Bancroft
Royce	Jason Beghe
C.O. Salem	Scott Wilson
Blondell	Lucinda Jenney
McCool	Morris Chestnut
Flea	Josh Hopkins
Slovnik	James Caviezel
Newberry	Angel David
Wickwire	Boyd Kestner
Instructor Pyro	Kevin Cage
Cortez	David Vadim
Miller	Gregg Bello
Chief of Staff	John Michael Higgins
Stamm	Steven Ramsey
Theodore Hayes	Daniel von Bargen
Instructor Johns	David Warshofsky

A bracingly gung-ho film for a nonmilitary-minded time, "G.I. Jane" is very entertaining get-tough fantasy with political and feminist underpinnings. After a number of respective career stumbles, co-producer/star Demi Moore and director Ridley Scott return to fine form here with a story that holds enormous appeal for women but also contains enough rough action and macho attitude to satisfy male auds. If Moore can regain public favor after turning off viewers with her last few features, this should score as a solid late-summer attraction.

Far from being "Private Benjamin," this is more like "Flashdance" in fatigues, a serious story of a capable and independent-minded woman who proves herself against tremendously difficult odds in the rigorous setting of Navy SEALs special training. Yarn could have gone astray in any number of ways, from the unintentionally comic to the merely cliched, but ends up putting itself over through an accumulation of highly charged challenges and confrontations, authentic-seeming details, tart dialogue, vibrant performances and credible emotions.

Opening reel sends up warning flares that an issue-driven tract could be in store. A tough-as-nails senator from Texas and senior member of the arms committee, Lillian DeHaven (Anne Bancroft), complaining loudly that one quarter of all military jobs remain off-limits to women, intimidates Navy brass into allowing a woman to train for the most elite of all operations units, the SEALs. Given the 60% dropout rate even among the highly qualified men who ordinarily apply, the secretary of the Navy agrees, figuring that whoever is selected will never make it anyway.

A candidate is soon found in Lt. Jordan O'Neil (Moore), a Naval intelligence officer who happens to be in pretty great shape. Leaving behind her fellow officer and boyfriend Royce (Jason Beghe) in Washington, D. C., O'Neil heads for training camp in Florida, where she is quickly plunged into Hell Week, an astonishingly grueling series of physical ordeals that the average person could never begin to endure.

O'Neil manages to survive the endless raft liftings, cold-water immersions, calisthenics and obstacle courses, but when she realizes that she is quietly being cut extra slack in some areas, she furiously demands the same full dose of punishment that the men receive. To further place herself on equal footing, she shaves her hair down to the requisite one-eighth of an inch and moves into the men's barracks, refusing to be deterred by the recruits' taunts and ridicule.

If one hasn't been until now, the viewer should be entirely on O'Neil's side by this point. As a black aspirant tells her, "You're just the new nigger on the block," and her deep underdog status demands almost super-human physical strength and emotional control, just as it allows no margin for error if she is to stay in the program.

Clearly interested in doing her no favors is the Command Master Chief (Viggo Mortensen), a tough taskmaster whose job it is to get in everyone's face and weed out those who can't cut it. O'Neil must also deal with an older commanding officer (Scott Wilson) who resents the meddling of politicians and the contemporary irritant known as sensitivity training, both of which are never far from his mind due to O'Neil's presence.

But just as O'Neil makes it through Hell Week and is sent off as the leader of a simulated commando mission, things become more complicated when it appears that Sen. DeHaven isn't at all sincere about wanted her handpicked guinea pig to make it through training: O'Neil, it seems, is just a disposable chess piece in a crafy politician's game.

The rigors of combat training, however, have well-prepared O'Neil to deal with the senator, and she manages to get herself reinstated in time to participate in a battle-readiness submarine operation in the Mediterranean that unexpectedly turns into an actual covert mission when trouble flares in Libya. Sooner than she ever imagined, O'Neil is put to the test under fire, with the Master Chief's life on the line.

Crucial to the film's success is the perfect match of style and content; pic is as hard, polished and powerfully functional as a newly cleaned gun. Dialogue scenes are highly compressed, going on at just the right length to make their points, and the emphasis on military jargon in David Twohy and Danielle Alexandra's keen-eared script makes for some extremely colorful exchanges; O'Neil enraged and vulgar rejoinder to the Master Chief upon being told to find a life somewhere else brings down the house and is bound to become a classic of its kind.

At the same time, Scott is very much on his game visually, as he reasserts his talent for visceral cinema by strongly conveying the physical aspects of arduous military training as well as the tension of actual battle. If logistically challenging war films ever come back into vogue, it would be good to see Scott try one.

"G. I. Jane" reps a recurrence in Scott's work of his strong sympathy for resourceful, ballsy women, first witnessed in "Alien" and most recently seen in "Thelma and Louise." Moore's tendency to take herself too seriously has been a problem in the past, but her fierce determination and humorless dedication she brings to her role are big pluses here, and she makes the exertion of O'Neil's will, and body, entirely believable. Physically, she looks as hard as any of the guys, and only the musicvideo-style shots of her feverishly doing one-armed push-ups smack of star ego and trendy body fetishizing.

Doing his best to steal the film, however, is Mortensen, who is terrific as the Master Chief who brings everyone to the brink. This fine actor has been an arresting presence in numerous films in recent years, but he cuts such a strong profile here that he may have found his breakthrough role.

The pleasure Bancroft takes in portraying an old-pro politician who excels at backroom deals proves contagious, Wilson is wonderfully understated in his important scenes as the base's c.o., and Lucinda Jenney brings an offbeat touch to her small role as the one female friend Jordan makes during training. The men in the unit are all convincing in attitude and physical ability.

Picture looks and sounds terrific, with lenser Hugh Johnson, production designer Arthur Max, editor Pietro Scalia and composer Trevor Jones making ace contributions.

–*Todd McCarthy*

Picture Credits

Pages ii and 121: Courtesy of The Paul M. Sammon Collection /
© 1996 Hollywood Pictures

Pages viii, 92, 137, 144 and 146: The Kobal Collection

Page 19: © 1965 British Film Institute

Page 33: Courtesy of Hovis

Page 47: Courtesy of The Paul M. Sammon Collection / © 1977
Paramount Pictures

Pages 57 and 135: The Paul M. Sammon Collection / © 1979 20th
Century Fox

Pages 68 and 71: The Paul M. Sammon Collection / © 1982 Warner
Brothers

Page 108 and 133: Photofest

Page 126: Courtesy of The Paul M. Sammon Collection / © 1997
Hollywood Pictures

Page 139: Courtesy of The Paul M. Sammon Collection / © 1985
Universal Pictures

Page 140: Courtesy of The Paul M. Sammon Collection / © 1987
Columbia Pictures

Page 142: Courtesy of The Paul M. Sammon Collection / © 1989
Paramount Pictures